I0037721

BROKEN SUPPLY CHAINS

How Financial Engineering Hollowed American Manufacturing and the Complex Journey to Resilience

By

Jeff Leimbach

Jeff Leimbach

"You cannot have a healthy economy without making things."

— *Andy Grove*, former Intel CEO

Jeff Leimbach

Table of Contents

Jeff Leimbach

Introduction

In March 2020, as the COVID-19 pandemic swept across the globe, America faced a stark reality: our supply chains were broken. Hospitals scrambled for protective equipment, consumers fought over basic necessities, and manufacturers struggled to source critical components. This crisis laid bare a vulnerability that had been building for decades, hidden beneath the surface of our seemingly robust economy.

The story of America's manufacturing decline is not just about offshoring or globalization. It's a tale of systematic dismantling, driven by financial engineering and short-term profit seeking. Take the case of Midwestern Manufacturing, once a thriving producer of medical equipment. After a private equity buyout, the company's assets were stripped, its workforce decimated, and its production moved overseas. When the pandemic hit, the factory stood empty, a ghost of its former self, unable to respond to the desperate need for ventilators.

This book uncovers the dual forces that have hollowed out our industrial base: global offshoring and domestic financial extraction. We'll explore how these trends have eroded what we call the "industrial commons" – the collective knowledge, skills, and infrastructure that once made American manufacturing a powerhouse.

Through in-depth analysis and compelling case studies, we'll examine the challenges of reshoring and the complex web of supply chain vulnerabilities. More importantly, we'll chart a course for renewal, offering a comprehensive roadmap to rebuild resilient and diversified supply networks.

The task ahead is daunting, but not insurmountable. By understanding the root causes of our manufacturing decline and embracing innovative solutions, we can restore America's industrial strength. This book is an invitation to business leaders, policymakers, investors, and concerned citizens to join in this critical mission. The future of our economy – and our nation – depends on it.

Chapter 1: The Great Unraveling

It was a chilly March morning in 2020, and dozens of cargo ships sat still off the coast of Los Angeles. They weren't moving, just floating there—fully loaded with electronics, clothing, auto parts—yet nothing was coming ashore. At the same time, shelves in grocery stores and pharmacies across the country were wiped clean. People scrambled for toilet paper, hand sanitizer, and canned goods. But it wasn't just everyday items that vanished. Critical components for ventilators, car engines, and medical devices also went missing. The pandemic hadn't just caused a temporary disruption. It showed, in the harshest way possible, just how fragile and hollowed-out America's manufacturing backbone had become.

For years, companies were told that "lean" was smart. Keep costs low, cut out waste, and don't tie up cash in inventory. The guiding principle was "Just-in-Time" (JIT)—a strategy made famous by Toyota, then taught like gospel in business schools. With JIT, parts were supposed to arrive right when they were needed. No stockpiles. No extras. It sounded efficient, and in a world where nothing went wrong, it was. Businesses saved money and shareholders got bigger returns.

But once the pandemic hit, that tight, no-margin-for-error system crumbled fast. A COVID outbreak at a single factory in Malaysia could suddenly stall production lines in Detroit. One ship getting stuck in the Suez Canal delayed products for weeks. Nurses in New York had to reuse protective masks because the global supply of medical gear had collapsed. What was once praised as sleek and brilliant now looked incredibly weak.

This wasn't bad luck. It was the result of decades of chasing cheaper production overseas. American companies didn't just move jobs—they moved entire networks of suppliers, expert workers, and even the machines used to make other machines. All of it in the name of squeezing out a few more dollars of profit. The real cost? We lost the ability to make essential things ourselves.

Here's one example that says it all: at the beginning of the pandemic, the U.S. made just 2% of the world's face masks. Almost all surgical and N95 masks were made overseas, mostly in China. When China stopped exporting to handle its own crisis, the mask supply dried up. And we couldn't ramp up quickly, because even the machines to make the mask-making machines were made abroad.

We hadn't just offshored labor—we had offshored know-how, tools, and control.

Some people called COVID-19 a black swan event—a rare disaster no one could see coming. But that's not really true. The virus didn't create new problems. It exposed ones we'd ignored for years. Long before the world knew the name SARS-CoV-2, American factories were shutting down, replaced by imports and warehouses. Towns that once revolved around metal shops or textile mills faded away. This wasn't just about China getting stronger or machines taking over. It was about choices—decisions made by CEOs and government leaders who bet everything on short-term gains.

A study in 2020 by the Reshoring Initiative found that between 1998 and 2017, the U.S. lost more than 70,000 factories. That number is real. Seventy thousand. In return, we got a worldwide web of supply chains stretching across oceans and continents. It all looked efficient, but it had no cushion, no backup plan. It only worked when everything worked. And when it didn't, the whole system buckled.

The cracks showed up quickly. In April 2020, General Motors had to shut down multiple plants because they couldn't get enough wiring harnesses from Mexico. Ford had to pause production of its best-selling F-

150 pickup due to a chip shortage. The losses added up fast. By late 2021, that single chip shortage was expected to cost the global auto industry $210 billion. Not million—billion. That's what happens when a supply chain breaks with no backup.

The chip shortage became the poster child for the problem. The U.S. invented the microchip and is home to companies like Intel. But by 2020, America was making just 12% of the world's semiconductors—down from 37% in 1990. Most of the cutting-edge chips came from Taiwan, mainly from one company: TSMC. When factories in Asia slowed down and demand for electronics soared, American companies had no choice but to wait and hope. They didn't have the ability to make the chips themselves anymore.

It wasn't just tech and masks. Medicine was affected too. Around 80% of the key ingredients in U.S. drugs come from overseas. When India, a major exporter of generic medicine, imposed limits on shipments, U.S. pharmacies began running low. It became painfully clear: if you don't control your own medicine supply, you can't protect your people during a crisis.

All of this led to one big, uncomfortable question: how did a country that once built tanks and planes by the thousands during World War II become unable to produce simple things like swabs and syringes? Part of the answer lies in the way we thought about manufacturing. For years, factories were seen as outdated—low-margin, low-prestige. The future, we were told, was in software, finance, and media. Let other countries make the stuff—we'd handle the ideas. It sounded modern and clean. But it was a risky illusion.

Another big factor? Financial tricks and cost-cutting. Instead of reinvesting in U.S. plants, companies poured money into stock buybacks and quick fixes to boost share prices. Take Boeing. Before the pandemic, it spent over $40 billion buying back its own stock, even while its production lines struggled. When COVID hit, the company needed government help just to stay afloat. That's the bitter irony: the very companies that had cut corners to look efficient were suddenly asking for bailouts when things went sideways.

What the pandemic made crystal clear was that chasing efficiency had made us weak. In trying to cut all the "waste," we'd gotten rid of the safety nets we needed in a crisis. We built a supply chain that was fast and cheap in good times, but one bad day away from falling apart.

To be fair, global trade isn't the enemy. It's lifted millions out of poverty and helped spread new ideas and technologies. But there's a huge difference between smart global partnerships and reckless overdependence. What we had created wasn't a strong, balanced global system. It was more like a teetering tower—one wrong move, and the whole thing toppled.

By the middle of 2020, these problems were hitting home. Parents couldn't find baby formula. Mechanics couldn't get car parts. Hospitals started rationing basic supplies like saline. This wasn't just annoying—it was dangerous. And in nearly every case, the reason was the same: we'd traded away resilience for short-term savings.

There's a word for systems like this: brittle. Brittle things don't bend—they snap. And when America's industrial strength was put to the test, it didn't hold. It broke.

When global trade ground to a halt in 2020, the breakdown didn't hit every industry the same way. Some areas struggled but kept going. Others slammed to a full stop. The biggest shock? How fast some of the most advanced, critical industries—ones we assumed were solid—completely buckled. What looked like a small delay in shipping was often a sign of something much deeper: a complete lack of capacity here at home. And when things broke, they didn't just inconvenience people—they froze entire industries in place.

Let's start with semiconductors. These tiny chips are the brains behind nearly every piece of modern tech—phones, computers, cars, planes, you name it. The U.S. was the birthplace of the semiconductor industry. Silicon Valley got its name because of this very thing. For decades, American giants like Intel, AMD, and Texas Instruments led the way in chip design and production. But in the 1990s, that started to change. Making chips was seen as expensive, complicated, and not very profitable. So companies began outsourcing the work to countries where labor was cheaper and regulations were looser.

By the time COVID hit, America's share of global semiconductor manufacturing had dropped to just 12%. And barely any of that was cutting-edge. The most advanced chips—the kind needed for new phones, advanced computers, and military tech—were being made almost entirely in Taiwan and South Korea. Taiwan's TSMC had become the main supplier, producing chips for everyone from Apple to U.S. defense contractors. It was an ironic twist: the U.S. had invented the technology, but decided it wasn't worth it to actually build the chips anymore.

So when people stuck at home started buying up electronics—and Asian factories faced their own COVID disruptions—U.S. companies had no cushion. Car makers were especially caught off guard. They had canceled chip orders early in the pandemic, betting that no one would be buying cars. But when demand came roaring back, they couldn't get the chips they needed. And this wasn't something money or favors could fix. The factories to make those chips didn't exist here anymore. Building one costs billions and takes years.

The fallout was immediate. Production lines shut down. Ford stopped making F-150 trucks. GM paused operations. Nissan started selling cars without navigation systems, just to get vehicles on the lot. All because of a $20 chip. One tiny missing part could keep a $40,000 car from being finished. It wasn't a cautionary tale—it was real, and it hurt.

Now look at the auto parts industry. Not exactly flashy, but it's the bloodstream of car manufacturing. A single vehicle can have around 30,000 parts, many of them made by highly specialized suppliers. Over time, the industry had turned its supply chain into a finely tuned machine. Just-in-time (JIT) manufacturing meant factories kept almost no inventory—parts arrived right when they were needed. That made things cheaper and more efficient, but also incredibly fragile.

In April 2020, GM had to shut down production because it couldn't get wiring harnesses from a supplier in Mexico. Nothing fancy—just basic parts needed to make a car run. But Mexico was in the middle of its own COVID outbreak, and the workers weren't showing up. There was no backup supplier. No plan B. The supply chain had become so optimized that there was no room for even the smallest hiccup.

And outsourcing wasn't just about saving on labor costs. It was also about making the company's balance sheet look better. Wall Street liked it when companies didn't own too many assets. So businesses sold off factories, got rid of tools, and leaned hard on suppliers to do the heavy lifting. It worked in good times. But when things got rough, those same companies had to call for government help—because they no longer had control over the things they needed most.

Then there's healthcare. Before 2020, hardly anyone thought about where hospital supplies came from. Masks, gloves, gowns, syringes—they were just always there. Until they weren't. In the early days of the pandemic, hospitals in cities like New York and Los Angeles were running out of N95 masks. Doctors had to reuse gear meant for one-time use. Some even wore garbage bags as makeshift gowns. This wasn't a shipping delay. The supply was gone.

Over 90% of surgical masks used in the U.S. were imported before COVID, mostly from China. The same went for gloves, gowns, and even the materials used to make them. Once the virus hit and demand exploded, countries like China, India, and Malaysia started keeping supplies for themselves. The U.S. had no backup.

And it wasn't just the finished products. Even the machines that made the machines—things like mask assembly lines—were foreign. You couldn't just open a new factory overnight. You needed special tools, trained workers, and a key material called melt-blown polypropylene, which acts as the filter in N95 masks. That material was only made in a few factories worldwide. The U.S. had almost none.

Hospitals also ran out of simple things like IV bags and saline. Shockingly, most of America's saline came from just one factory in Puerto Rico, which had already been damaged during Hurricane Maria in 2017. Even after that disaster, the system didn't change. Why? Because building in redundancy—having backups—was seen as a waste of money.

One hospital official said it best: "We were one flat tire away from catastrophe." The whole system had been running on thin margins, betting that nothing major would go wrong. That wasn't smart planning. It was wishful thinking.

Looking at all of this, a clear pattern shows up. These weren't random accidents. They were the result of how whole industries were built—not for stability, but for short-term savings. The U.S. economy was running on the belief that global trade would always work smoothly, that overseas partners would always cooperate, and that serious disruptions were rare. That belief didn't hold up when the real test came.

Offshoring was only part of the problem. The deeper issue was how businesses started thinking about risk, investment, and what really mattered. We didn't just stop making stuff. We let the skills, the tools, and the systems behind making stuff disappear. Training programs shut down. Skilled workers retired, and no one replaced them. Old factories were torn down or turned into condos and data centers.

Whether it was semiconductors, car parts, or medical supplies, the problem wasn't just that we were global. It was that we had made our systems too thin, too fragile, and too focused on squeezing out every last cent. There was no strength left—just a skeleton. And when pressure hit, the bones cracked.

One executive from a Midwest auto parts company said it plainly: "We outsourced everything but the liability." They still owned the brands and the contracts. But when it came time to deliver the goods, they couldn't.

What's really alarming is how fast everything fell apart once the conditions changed. This wasn't a slow decline. By April 2020, companies were flying in parts on private jets. By May, governors were making cold calls to mask suppliers in China. By June, firms were scouring eBay for used factory machines. It was a full-blown emergency—not caused by war or sabotage, but by the choices we made ourselves.

And at the root of it all? A lack of slack. No wiggle room. An obsession with efficiency that made us blind to the need for resilience. If something didn't pay off right away, it got cut. Until the moment we desperately needed it.

Three different industries. One shared failure. Each one had been stripped down to its most cost-efficient version—and each one collapsed when the world changed. The truth isn't that we were caught off guard. It's that we built the whole system to be unready.

When people talk about the fall of American manufacturing, the usual story sounds familiar: blame globalization. Foreign factories with cheaper labor and looser rules undercut U.S. companies. Corporations chased lower costs abroad. The American economy shifted toward services and tech.

That's the version we've heard for years—and there's definitely some truth to it. But it's only part of the picture.

The rest of the story is harder to hear— and it happened right here at home. It wasn't just what went on overseas. It was decisions made in American boardrooms and investment firms. It was Wall Street's influence and the rise of corporate strategies that treated factories like burdens instead of assets. What hollowed out U.S. manufacturing wasn't only outside pressure. It was also a series of homegrown choices—financial moves, business trends, and policy decisions that chipped away at our own industrial backbone.

To really understand how we got here, we have to see through both lenses: one looking outward at trade deals and offshoring, and the other inward at how American businesses and policymakers helped weaken the very system they claimed to support. These two forces didn't act separately—they fed off each other in a loop that made things worse over time.

Let's begin with the global side.

By the late 1900s, the push for worldwide economic integration had strong support across political lines. Deals like NAFTA and the opening of trade with China were sold as big wins. The idea was simple: consumers would get cheaper goods, U.S.

companies would gain access to huge markets, and the world would become more connected. Economists praised the benefits—lower costs, more efficiency, global supply chains. On paper, it all looked smart.

But what actually happened was more one-sided. America sent jobs abroad and brought back finished products. Entire industries packed up and moved to Mexico, China, or Southeast Asia. Places that once thrived on manufacturing were left behind. Just between 2000 and 2010, the U.S. lost over five million manufacturing jobs—many of them tied to China's rise as the world's go-to factory.

Look at textiles. In the 1960s, the American South was full of busy textile mills. By the early 2000s, many of those mills had shut down. Jobs went to countries where wages were far lower. The same thing happened in steel, furniture, electronics—even advanced tech components like batteries and semiconductors.

But when jobs left, it wasn't just people who were impacted. Entire systems collapsed. Supplier networks, technical training, and hands-on engineering expertise faded away. These were the pieces that kept U.S. manufacturing strong, and once they disappeared, they were incredibly hard to bring back.

Still, it's not like American companies just suddenly decided to move production abroad for no reason. That shift was pushed along by something else: pressure from inside.

And that brings us to the domestic side of the story—the part that rarely gets enough attention.

Starting in the 1980s and really picking up in the 1990s, a new idea took over corporate America: the mission of a company was no longer to serve customers, employees, and communities equally. It was to boost stock prices and reward shareholders—fast.

That thinking led to something called "financial engineering."

It sounds technical, but it really comes down to playing with money to make a company look more profitable, even if it's not actually becoming stronger. This could mean buying back stock, loading up on debt, cutting jobs, or outsourcing key parts of the business. The goal was to do less, own less, and just skim off the top.

Factories were seen as expensive headaches. Workers were viewed as unpredictable. Equipment was considered a financial drag. So instead of building things in-house, companies outsourced. Instead of training workers, they trimmed headcounts. The focus shifted to branding, design, and marketing—the "lighter" parts of business that didn't require messy investments in plants and people.

Consultants and banks loved this approach. They promoted it as the smart, efficient way to run a company. CEOs were rewarded for cutting costs, not building for the future. The numbers that mattered were things like return on equity and earnings per share—metrics that told you how well the stock was doing, not how strong the company actually was.

And this wasn't a fringe movement—it reshaped entire industries.

Take the auto industry. By the early 2000s, many American carmakers had sold off their in-house parts divisions. Wall Street said vertical integration—making things yourself—was old-fashioned. It was better to focus on final assembly and outsource the rest. That might have looked good on spreadsheets, but it left companies dangerously exposed.

So when COVID hit, and the supply chains broke down, those automakers couldn't get the parts they needed. The system had been fragile all along. The pandemic just made it obvious.

It's easy to say all this was just bad luck or poor forecasting. But a lot of people at the top knew exactly what they were doing. Their goal wasn't long-term stability—it was to pull out as much money as possible while the business still looked good.

Just look at stock buybacks. Back in 1982, the SEC changed the rules to make them easier. Since then, they've exploded in popularity. In recent years, big companies have spent more buying back their own stock than on hiring workers, building new facilities, or investing in research. These buybacks helped stock prices rise—great for shareholders, but not so great for the company's actual future.

Or consider private equity. These firms buy up manufacturing businesses, saddle them with debt, cut spending, and then try to flip them for a profit. They often gut the very things that make a business sustainable: skilled workers, reliable machinery, strong supply chains. The company might look leaner, but it's actually weaker.

One of the most telling examples is Simmons Bedding Company. Once a respected American brand, it got passed around from one private equity firm to another. With each sale came more debt, more cuts, and less investment in the actual business. By the time the 2008 crisis hit, Simmons couldn't meet demand or maintain quality. The name is still around, but the real company behind it was stripped down and broken.

And here's the thing: none of this was hidden. Business schools taught these strategies. Financial media praised them. Executives were paid to follow them. It wasn't a fluke—it was the standard playbook.

Meanwhile, government policy often made things worse. Tax breaks encouraged this kind of behavior. Antitrust rules weren't enforced. Trade policies favored global sourcing over domestic strength. There was no real plan for how to protect or grow key industries. The idea was, let the market decide. Until the market failed.

Today, we're left with the result: a country that leads in ideas but struggles to make the things it invents. We've got top universities and innovative startups, but our factories are fewer, and our industrial workforce is shrinking. We dominate in finance, but we depend on other countries for critical goods.

This didn't just happen. It was built into the system.

So fixing it isn't just about bringing back a few factories or giving out tax cuts. We have to deal with both sides of the problem. That means facing the realities of global trade— but also questioning the corporate incentives that made it so easy to send jobs and skills overseas.

Manufacturing shouldn't be treated like a leftover from the past. It's not just about bringing back blue-collar jobs. It's about keeping the ability to make what we invent, to manage our own supply chains, and to stay strong in the face of global shocks.

To get there, we'll need to look hard at the rules we've set for our own companies. That means rethinking how we define success—moving away from short-term stock gains and toward long-term strength. It means asking better questions. Not just, "How do we cut costs?" but "How do we build something that lasts?"

This isn't about turning back the clock. It's about understanding what really happened—both abroad and at home—so we can make smarter choices going forward.

Because the next crisis won't give us time to play catch-up.

Jeff Leimbach

Chapter 2: Beyond Offshoring: The Extraction Economy

Start talking about the decline of American manufacturing, and it won't take long for someone to blame offshoring. Factories closing and heading to China, call centers popping up in India, machines crated up in Michigan and reassembled in Vietnam—these are the images most people picture. Offshoring is easy to see. It comes with big headlines, political slogans, and stacks of shipping containers. But there's another, quieter force that's done just as much—maybe more—damage. It's not just about where the work went. It's about what was done to the heart of American business itself.

Let's talk about extraction.

Now, when you hear "extraction," you might think of mining or oil drilling. But here, it means something different: the practice of pulling value out of a business without putting anything back in. It's a kind of slow bleed—where companies aren't focused on building or growing, but on cutting, selling, and cashing out. This isn't about moving jobs overseas. It's about gutting what's left behind.

Offshoring is a strategy. Extraction is a mindset.

To understand how we got here, we need to look back. The usual story starts in the 1970s and ramps up through the '80s and '90s: U.S. companies began shifting production overseas to cut costs and stay competitive. Unions got weaker, factory towns crumbled, and "Made in the USA" started to fade. That story's true—but it's not the full picture.

Because many of those decisions weren't really about efficiency or competition. They were about keeping stock prices high, impressing investors, and paying off debt. Offshoring was often the result—not the cause—of a bigger issue. The real driving force? Financial tactics designed to squeeze quick gains, no matter the long-term cost.

This is the heart of extraction. Instead of building better products or reaching new customers, companies cut spending, sold off assets, laid off workers, and slashed research budgets. It was about wringing as much money as possible from a company—even if it meant hollowing it out.

So while offshoring is a logistical move, extraction is a way of thinking. One that prioritizes quick wins over long-term health.

The timing is important too. Yes, globalization picked up speed in the '70s and '80s. But the deep cuts to U.S. industry happened later—during the economic boom of the 1990s and early 2000s. That was when many companies didn't just lose to global competition—they gave up on competing at all. They started walking away from making things entirely.

Look at the electronics industry. In 1995, America still had a strong foothold in semiconductor manufacturing. By 2005, much of that had vanished—not because other countries beat us, but because U.S. firms sold their factories, outsourced their work, and shifted to "fabless" models. They didn't lose ground. They cashed out.

Or take textiles. American apparel companies didn't disappear overnight. They were picked apart. Regional brands were snapped up by conglomerates, sewing jobs were sent abroad, and suppliers were pushed to the brink. The driving force wasn't always competition—it was often private equity. These firms saw value in real estate, brands, and cheap labor, and moved quickly to extract it.

It's easy to chalk all this up to globalization. But globalization is just the setting. Extraction is the motive.

And the numbers help tell the story.

Between 1982 and 2000, U.S. manufacturing productivity rose by about 3% a year, according to the Bureau of Labor Statistics. That means factories were getting better and more efficient. But during that same time, over 2 million manufacturing jobs disappeared. Automation alone doesn't explain that drop. A 2018 MIT study found that only about 13% of the job losses from 1999 to 2011 were due to trade with China. So what caused the rest?

The answer lies in how companies were run. Business leaders, under pressure to deliver fast returns, stopped thinking long-term. Why spend money to modernize a factory when you could outsource and boost profits right away? Why invest in innovation when cutting jobs made your stock go up?

On paper, it looked like smart business. But in reality, it often meant companies were cutting into their own core. There's a big difference between getting lean and cutting into your muscle—and by the 2000s, many firms were cutting into bone.

One of the clearest examples of this is Sears.

Once a retail powerhouse with a huge supply chain, in-house brands, and its own credit system, Sears was what Amazon is today. But after hedge fund manager Eddie Lampert took over, the company didn't crash all at once. It fell apart piece by piece. Lampert sold off Sears' real estate, its brands, and starved its stores of investment. All under the banner of "unlocking value." But once all that "value" was unlocked and sold off, there was nothing left. No stores, no growth, no company.

That's what extraction looks like.

And Sears isn't alone. This same model has played out in countless other industries. A private equity firm buys a tool manufacturer, loads it with debt, then pays itself a fat dividend—that's extraction. A public company slashes research spending to boost the stock and pay out bonuses—that's extraction too. Even when consultants tell big firms to get rid of their "non-core" assets—the parts that actually make things—that's another form of it.

Sometimes offshoring and extraction went hand in hand. Companies would justify cuts and sell-offs by pointing to globalization. "We're moving to Asia to stay competitive" sounded better than "We're firing our team and selling our patents." But either way, the end result was the same: America lost the ability—and the will—to make things.

And this kind of damage doesn't always make the news. It's not always a shuttered factory or a massive layoff. Sometimes it's quieter. A young engineer doesn't get hired. A small supplier gets squeezed too hard and closes. A company with a proud history becomes nothing more than a name and a few trademarks, held by an investment firm.

Here's the uncomfortable part: many of these wounds weren't inflicted by outside forces. They came from inside—from decisions made in boardrooms and investment offices, from Wall Street to Silicon Valley.

So, if we boil it down to one idea: offshoring sent the jobs away. Extraction made the jobs disappear in the first place.

That difference matters. Not just for understanding the past, but for shaping what comes next. If we treat the decline of American industry as only a trade problem, we'll reach for trade tools—tariffs, subsidies, reshoring plans. But if the deeper issue is extraction, we need a different approach—one that addresses how companies are run, how they measure success, and what kind of future we're actually building.

For years, we've tried to bring manufacturing back without facing the business culture that sees factories as burdens and engineers as expenses. Until we do, every effort to rebuild will face the same uphill battle—fighting against a system that doesn't value the very things we're trying to restore.

Because this didn't all start with globalization. It started when we decided that making money off a company mattered more than what the company actually made.

Step into a business school classroom in the late 1960s, and the conversations would sound pretty familiar: talk of growth, product development, long-term strategy, and balancing the needs of employees, customers, and shareholders. Back then, reinvesting profits back into the company wasn't just encouraged—it was expected. Businesses were seen as living institutions, focused on building, expanding, and supporting the communities around them.

But by the 1980s and '90s, something had clearly changed. The language had become colder, more technical. Acronyms like ROIC and EBITDA took center stage. Phrases like "margin enhancement" and "creating shareholder value" replaced talk of mission and innovation. It wasn't just new jargon—it was a new way of thinking. Companies were no longer seen as communities or engines of innovation. They were viewed more like financial machines: something to be tuned, stripped down, or even flipped for profit.

This shift didn't happen all at once, but when it hit, it moved fast. And it left a trail behind: R&D budgets slashed, supply chains hollowed out, apprenticeships disappearing, and factories becoming just another line item to cut.

One of the biggest turning points in this shift was a change in corporate strategy—from "retain and reinvest" to "downsize and distribute."

After World War II, from about 1945 to the mid-1970s, most big companies followed the retain-and-reinvest model. They held onto their earnings and used them to buy better equipment, open new plants, train workers, and design new products. That helped the company grow stronger and lifted up the economy around it. The system wasn't perfect—far from it—but the basic idea was that business success should feed future growth, not just pad someone's pocket.

But as financial markets gained influence, that idea started to fade. By the 1980s, a new generation of leaders emerged—many with MBAs and a focus on turning companies into sleek, efficient, return-generating machines. They weren't just being greedy—they were following a new playbook. This mindset was reinforced by Wall Street, consulting firms, and investors who wanted results—and fast.

A big part of the change came from how success was measured. One of the most popular tools was Return on Invested Capital (ROIC), which tracks how effectively a company turns investments into profit. On paper, that seems reasonable. But when ROIC becomes the main goal, it can twist priorities.

Imagine you run a company that makes heavy machinery. To raise your ROIC, you could invest in new equipment, launch a new product line, and train workers. That might take years. Or, you could just sell off equipment, outsource the work, lay off half your team, and use the money to buy back your stock. That's a fast bump in ROIC—with none of the long-term effort.

And that's the real issue: these financial metrics tend to reward shrinking, not growing. They push companies toward asset-light models, fewer workers, and lower capital spending. In that world, building things becomes a problem instead of a strength.

Take EBITDA—short for Earnings Before Interest, Taxes, Depreciation, and Amortization. It became a kind of magic number. When private equity firms looked at EBITDA, it was like saying, "Let's pretend this business has no real-world costs and just focus on the money it generates." But the real world doesn't work that way. Machines break down. Workers need training. New ideas take time to develop. EBITDA ignores all that. It makes companies look stronger on paper than they really are.

The more these numbers took over, the more they changed how companies behaved. Investing in new tools or launching long-term projects suddenly seemed risky.

Why spend money today for a return five years from now, when you could fire workers and boost profits next quarter?

And then came stock-based executive pay.

Starting in the 1980s, and really picking up in the 1990s, CEOs were increasingly paid in stock—options, restricted shares, performance bonuses. The goal was to tie their success to the company's success. But in practice, it meant executives could get rich by pumping up the stock price in the short term, even if it hurt the company down the road.

Want your stock price to jump? Announce layoffs. Cut spending. Buy back shares. The market loves it. The price goes up, and so does your paycheck. Whether the company is healthier doesn't really matter—especially if you're planning to leave before the damage shows.

Then came the activist investors. These weren't the old-school board members who knew the company inside and out. They were often hedge funds that bought big stakes, demanded changes, and pushed for quick payoffs. That usually meant spinning off divisions, cutting costs, and sending money back to shareholders.

Helping all of this along were the management consultants. Armed with sharp suits and slick presentations, they told companies to focus on their "core competencies" and cut the rest. That sounded smart, but often meant getting rid of the very things that built the company in the first place—like manufacturing plants, training departments, or testing labs. Why own a factory when you can outsource it and show better margins?

By the late '90s, this approach was seen as brilliant. CEOs were praised for getting "lean." Case studies celebrated companies that sold off their manufacturing arms. Wall Street analysts gave high marks to firms with no physical footprint. Consultants promised that trimming operations would boost ROIC. The message was clear: don't build—extract.

One former tech executive summed it up perfectly: "We were told that real estate, R&D, even our own engineers were 'non-core.' The core, apparently, was the brand and the balance sheet."

In that mindset, manufacturing became a problem. Factories were expensive, complicated, and tied up capital. Better to move production offshore, cut the headcount, and collect the savings.

Even companies that kept some production in-house began to act differently. Long-term plans got shelved. Upgrades were postponed. Apprenticeship programs were canceled. Engineers were replaced by temporary contractors. And when the economy turned sour, those already-weakened operations were first to go.

What made this all so dangerous was how quietly it happened. You didn't always see it in dramatic headlines or sudden factory closures. It showed up as slow decay: machines not maintained, patents not filed, younger workers not trained. A company could still show solid earnings even as it was slowly losing its edge. By the time the damage became obvious, the executives had already moved on—stock options cashed out, golden parachutes deployed.

There's a kind of twisted brilliance to it: take a strong, productive business and turn it into a short-term cash machine. It works—for a while. You cut costs, juice the numbers, watch the stock price soar. And then you leave someone else to deal with the mess: the laid-off workers, the hollowed-out towns, the lost skills.

And the impact doesn't stop with the companies. When manufacturing fades, the whole ecosystem suffers. Local suppliers disappear. Skilled jobs vanish. Fewer kids go into engineering. Colleges shrink their technical programs. The ability to build complex things starts to vanish—not because someone beat us—but because we decided it wasn't worth the trouble.

Now, to be clear, there's nothing wrong with using metrics like ROIC or EBITDA. When used properly, they can help businesses stay lean and focused. But when those numbers become the only thing that matters, they twist priorities. They make it seem like the goal isn't to build something lasting, but to squeeze as much value out as quickly as possible—before the whole thing falls apart.

That's really the story of American industry over the last forty years: a shift from creating to extracting, from investing patiently to chasing fast returns. Companies that once saw themselves as pillars of the economy became tools for quick payouts. The factory floor got replaced by the spreadsheet.

And maybe the hardest part? We told ourselves this was smart. Strategic. Visionary.

But the truth is, a lot of what passed for strategy was just a slow, quiet dismantling—of companies, of communities, and of the country's industrial strength. It made for nice earnings reports and stock windfalls. But when the real crisis hit, there was nothing left to fall back on.

Case Study I: The Hollowing of a Midwest Electronics Manufacturer

The first thing you'd notice about MidTech Instruments wasn't the factory itself—

it was the parking lot. Every weekday morning, rows of dusty pickup trucks and well-worn sedans filled the lot by 7 a.m. Workers shuffled in for the first shift, some sipping vending machine coffee, others lacing up their steel-toed boots or zipping up their windbreakers with the MidTech logo stitched on the chest. The building sat just outside Dayton, Ohio—a low, windowless structure that looked more like a high school gym than the heart of a high-tech operation. But inside, MidTech was building some of the most precise electronics in the country.

The company was founded in the 1960s by two former aerospace engineers. It wasn't flashy, but it had earned deep respect in its field. MidTech specialized in analog signal processing—components that helped medical equipment, sonar systems, and aircraft electronics run reliably and clearly. If you needed low-noise amplifiers or phase-locked loops that stayed rock solid, MidTech was the go-to. They built a reputation for high performance and quick turnaround. A client could call from across the country with a last-minute design change, and MidTech could have a prototype ready in a matter of days. They had their own in-house engineering team, testing lab, machine shop, and even a small but advanced clean room. The profits weren't huge, but the business was solid, dependable, and built to last.

By the late '90s, MidTech had grown to about 500 employees. They weren't a household name, but they had a strong presence in the medical, telecom, and defense sectors. Their parts went into everything from defibrillators to aircraft radios to industrial control systems. They held a tidy portfolio of patents, mostly small tweaks and improvements, but meaningful ones. Their most valuable patent was a specialized filter that reduced signal noise at high frequencies without draining too much power—a big win for portable medical devices. This intellectual property helped them land long-term contracts and fend off bigger competitors.

The company's leadership was careful and steady. They reinvested profits into operations, kept control of their own tooling, and funded a modest R&D team that still managed to innovate. Veteran engineers worked closely with the folks on the shop floor, adjusting designs in real time and fine-tuning production runs. That tight connection between design and manufacturing helped them move quickly without cutting corners. It wasn't a glamorous business, but it was good work, and people were proud of it.

So when a private equity firm—let's call them Crestwood Capital—announced in 2003 that they were acquiring MidTech in a leveraged buyout, people felt a mix of curiosity and cautious hope. Crestwood said all the right things. They talked about helping MidTech grow, making strategic improvements, and "unlocking value." They promised not to move the factory or shake things up too much. A local business journal ran a short piece on the deal, saying Crestwood had a solid track record with industrial firms.

But not long after, things started to change.

First came the debt.

Crestwood had borrowed most of the money to buy MidTech, and now the company itself was responsible for paying that debt back. Instead of using profits to invest in the business, MidTech now had to use most of its earnings to make interest payments. On paper, nothing had changed. But in reality, the company had far less room to breathe. Every quarter, more cash was funneled into debt service.

Next came the real estate deal.

Crestwood arranged for MidTech to sell its factory building—a property they'd owned outright for years—and lease it back. It was pitched as a way to raise cash. But it meant MidTech went from being its own landlord to paying rent, with costs that would only increase over time. What used to be an asset became a monthly liability.

Then came the cuts.

The R&D budget was slashed by nearly half. Projects that weren't seen as immediately profitable were canceled. Several long-time engineers left—some retired early, some went to competitors, one started teaching. These weren't just workers; they held years of hands-on knowledge, the kind that doesn't get written down. Their replacements were younger, cheaper, and less experienced—often contract workers unfamiliar with the company's culture or products.

Design and prototyping work was outsourced to a firm in Bangalore. It saved money upfront, no doubt. But it also slowed everything down. When a problem popped up on the production line, it used to be that an engineer could just walk over and help fix it. Now, issues had to be documented, emailed across time zones, and fit into someone else's schedule. MidTech's trademark speed and flexibility started to fade.

Meanwhile, the company's most valuable patents—including that filter design—were sold to a licensing company. The plan was for MidTech to license the technology back and focus on production. But in reality, they gave up one of their biggest competitive edges. Now, any rival with enough cash could use the same design. What had once protected them was now just another revenue stream—for someone else.

By 2007, things were slowing down. Sales flattened. Quality dipped. Orders shipped late. Customer support wasn't what it used to be. Long-time clients, especially in the medical field, started quietly looking for other suppliers. Defense contractors, who depended on rock-solid reliability, stopped including MidTech in new bids. Morale on the factory floor sank. Layoffs hit. Retirement benefits were trimmed. The company picnic was canceled. Even the snacks in the vending machine got cheaper. No one thing broke the business—it was death by a thousand cuts.

Then came the final move.

In 2009, Crestwood split off MidTech's most profitable customer contracts—mostly long-term accounts with recurring revenue—and sold them to a Texas-based competitor. The deal was done through a holding company, structured to avoid taxes and boost short-term gains. What remained of MidTech—stripped of its IP and best clients—was declared unprofitable. The company was liquidated in early 2010.

There was no big headline. No dramatic collapse. Just a short notice that the factory was closing and that severance would be limited. The machines were sold off at auction. The building, once a hub of skilled work, became a warehouse for auto parts. Within a few months, you couldn't tell MidTech had ever been there.

But this wasn't a story of failure—not in the usual sense. MidTech didn't fall behind in technology. It didn't get crushed by cheap imports. It wasn't bloated or mismanaged. It was a solid, well-run company with a strong product and a skilled team. But to its new owners, it was worth more in pieces than as a whole.

And that's the hard part to swallow.

MidTech didn't die from competition— it was dismantled, bit by bit, for profit. The factory, the workers, the engineering brainpower—they weren't considered assets. They were ignored or treated as expenses that got in the way of the real goal: maximizing returns.

This wasn't a one-off. It was part of a pattern.

Crestwood didn't break the law. They didn't steal or commit fraud. They followed the playbook of modern financial engineering: load the company with debt, sell off its parts, cut costs, and extract value. And by that measure, they succeeded. Their investors made money. The deal was a financial win.

But for the people in Dayton—the workers, the suppliers, the community—it was a loss that kept rippling outward. Hundreds of jobs were gone. A machine shop that made enclosures for MidTech shut down. The local community college dropped its electronics program. A daycare across the street from the plant closed its doors.

What happened to MidTech wasn't unusual. It's happening all over. And it shows something deeper: the shift from seeing companies as builders of products to seeing them as bundles of assets to be mined. In this view, factories, workers, and research aren't the future—they're costs to be trimmed or sold off.

The scariest part? From the outside, a company like MidTech can look fine for years. The lights are still on. Orders are still going out. The website still works. But inside, the heart is gone. The engineers are gone. The innovation has stopped. The future has been sold off piece by piece.

We often hear that manufacturing jobs are vanishing because of automation, trade, or regulation. But MidTech's story points to something else: a quiet, calculated decision to cash out, even if it means killing the company in the process. It's not a market failure—it's a strategy.

There's a big difference between selling products and selling the ability to make them. One builds something lasting. The other burns it down for parts. MidTech didn't just get unlucky. It got hollowed out—on purpose. And in that empty shell, you can hear the echo of a much bigger story.

Jeff Leimbach

Chapter 3: The Private Equity Playbook

In the summer of 1983, a quiet headline appeared in The Wall Street Journal: "Textron Sells Division in $200 Million Leveraged Buyout." At the time, few people noticed or cared. Buyouts were niche deals—technical financial maneuvers that rarely made waves outside of Wall Street. But for those paying close attention, this was a sign that something was shifting. A new kind of business thinking was starting to take root, one that would soon reshape American manufacturing.

The traditional model of industry—build great products, invest in skilled workers, and beat competitors through quality and innovation—was about to be challenged by something faster and far more aggressive. This new model didn't focus on how well a company made its products. It focused on how much money could be pulled from it.

By the late 1980s, Wall Street had figured out that manufacturing firms made perfect targets for a strategy called the leveraged buyout, or LBO. But these weren't casual investors. These were private equity firms, armed with piles of cash and a new playbook. Instead of buying companies with their own money, they borrowed most of the funds, then handed the debt to the company they just bought. It's like buying a house and making the house pay off the mortgage—and expecting the kitchen to foot the bill.

That may sound absurd outside the world of finance, but it's exactly how these deals work. Picture a family-owned metal shop that's been around for 70 years, with 800 employees and a solid reputation in the aerospace supply chain. A private equity firm decides to buy it, putting up just 30% of the money and borrowing the rest. Then they shift that debt onto the company's books. Overnight, a once-stable manufacturer is buried under millions in loans it never asked for. Now, instead of focusing on growing or improving, its top priority is paying down debt.

Private equity loves this setup because it amplifies their potential profits. If they only invest 30% of the purchase price but walk away with 100% of the gains, their returns skyrocket—assuming the company survives. If it doesn't? Their risk is capped at that 30%, while the banks and bondholders eat the losses. This lopsided risk-reward structure encourages bold, sometimes reckless decisions. And when this mindset spreads across industries, the risks stop being individual—they become systemic.

None of this happened by chance. The conditions that made leveraged buyouts so common were created. Starting in the late 1970s and speeding up in the Reagan era, the financial sector was loosened up. Regulations were peeled back, antitrust laws were relaxed, tax rules were tweaked to favor debt over equity, and interest rates dropped, making borrowing easier. At the same time, a new idea started gaining traction in corporate boardrooms: shareholder primacy. The belief that a company's only real goal should be to maximize returns for its shareholders. Not to build great products. Not to create good jobs. Just make the stock price go up.

In this environment, manufacturing companies—with their factories, equipment, and land—looked like treasure chests. Unlike software startups or consulting firms, they had real assets you could borrow against. You could mortgage a building. Sell off machines and lease them back. Cut research budgets or postpone maintenance to boost profits for a few quarters. These companies had been designed to last. Private equity came in with a stopwatch.

By 2023, private equity firms owned or controlled companies that employed around 10% of the U.S. workforce. But their influence reaches even further. While headlines tend to focus on flashy deals in retail or healthcare, the heart of their activity is often in mid-sized manufacturing—an area that doesn't usually make the news. These are the quiet companies Americans rely on every day without realizing it: bolt makers in Ohio, plastics processors in Indiana, circuit board shops in Wisconsin. They're the backbone of U.S. industry.

These mid-sized firms—usually with $50 million to $1 billion in revenue—form most of the country's industrial supply chain. They're crucial not just because of what they produce, but because of how they help other industries move forward. Sectors like aerospace, automotive, and medical technology all depend on them. But that same importance makes them easy targets for financial playbooks.

Part of their vulnerability lies in how they're structured. They don't have the resources that large public companies do. They don't have big legal teams or access to cheap loans. Many are still run by families or local managers nearing retirement, after decades of steady work. They're attractive because they're stable, rich in physical assets, and often not "optimized" in financial terms— exactly the kind of profile that private equity looks for.

The sales pitch from private equity sounds impressive. They say they'll "modernize" operations, find "hidden value," and improve "efficiency." But behind the buzzwords is a much simpler aim: get cash out, fast. Most private equity firms work on a tight timeline—usually 3 to 7 years. That means they need to buy, restructure, and resell the company in that short window, ideally with big profits. There's no reason for them to think about what happens 10 or 15 years down the road. The pressure is always on the short-term.

And that's a serious problem for manufacturing. These companies thrive on long timelines—planning and investing for the next decade, not the next quarter. They need time to train workers, upgrade machines, and develop new products. Private equity can't wait that long. So corners get cut. Equipment upgrades are put off. Maintenance gets delayed. Engineering and training teams are downsized. Instead of being part of a healthy, long-term system, the company becomes a tool for squeezing out quick profits.

To be fair, not every private equity deal ends badly. Some firms really do bring better management, new technology, or access to bigger markets. But the overall pattern leans more toward draining than building. A Harvard Business School study found that private equity-owned manufacturing firms were more likely to lay off workers, close plants, and slash R&D spending than those owned by other types of investors. When gains happen, they tend to benefit a small group of insiders. The costs—lost jobs, weaker communities, frayed supply chains—are spread out across the rest of us.

What's most unsettling is how routine this model has become. For many manufacturers, being bought by a private equity firm is just another step in their life cycle. Industry publications cover these deals like they're nothing new. Trade shows host panels on how to work with PE partners. Business schools teach financial engineering as a standard tool. And one number has become the yardstick for success: EBITDA—earnings before interest, taxes, depreciation, and amortization.

But EBITDA doesn't tell you if a factory roof is leaking. It doesn't tell you whether the machines are falling behind, or whether the next generation of skilled workers is being trained. It's just a number that shows short-term cash flow. Still, it's the number private equity cares about most—because that's what helps them sell the company for a higher price than they paid. That's the game.

And the game has real consequences. When the companies making parts for submarines or medical gear are managed for short-term cash rather than long-term strength, the risks go beyond the factory floor. They touch national security. They shape our ability to handle emergencies, innovate, and protect critical technologies. Financial engineering may seem invisible, but its effects are everywhere in the slow erosion of America's industrial backbone.

You won't see it in national job numbers. But you'll feel it when a town loses its last tool shop, or when a factory that once made aircraft parts in Michigan starts shipping cheap packaging from Mexico. You'll see it when people work hard but don't see the rewards.

Private equity's rise in manufacturing wasn't an accident. It didn't appear overnight. It happened bit by bit—deal by deal, spreadsheet by spreadsheet. What was once a world driven by engineering skill has been overtaken by financial logic built on debt and fast exits. The language has changed, but the story remains the same: take as much as you can now, and let someone else deal with the fallout later.

For the people still working in the heart of American manufacturing, the question isn't whether private equity will come knocking. It's what happens once it walks through the door.

Anatomy of a Buyout – The Precision Machining Case

When you walked into TriCraft Precision back in 2010, the first thing you felt was the sound. The hum of milling machines, the hiss of air drills, the steady clatter of CNC lathes—it wasn't noise, it was rhythm. It sounded like people who knew exactly what they were doing. About 80 machinists, engineers, and technicians moved through the shop with quiet focus. Most had been there for decades. This wasn't just a job for them. It was a craft.

TriCraft sat in a quiet industrial park in western Pennsylvania, surrounded by chain-link fences and faded signage from the 1950s. It had been around since 1957, making tight-tolerance parts for aerospace and defense companies. The company didn't make headlines, but it didn't miss deadlines either. In the supply chain world, that was enough to build a reputation: deliver what you promise, no drama.

At that point, TriCraft was still run by the Collins family. Frank Collins, the founder's son, had started on the shop floor and worked his way up to president. After a lifetime in the business, he was ready to retire and had started looking at offers. Buyers had been circling for years—competitors, big defense firms, strategic buyers. But in 2011, he finally said yes to a private equity group called Harding Tate Capital.

On paper, the deal looked good. TriCraft was valued just under $90 million. Harding Tate put in about $27 million of its own cash. The rest? Borrowed. Bank loans, high-yield bonds—around $63 million in total debt, which was immediately shifted onto TriCraft's books. Overnight, the company went from debt-free to deeply leveraged.

At first, nobody on the shop floor noticed. The machines kept running, the lights stayed on, and paychecks showed up on schedule. But in the boardroom, everything had changed.

Harding Tate didn't wait around. In the first quarter, they kicked off a "strategic efficiency review." Out went Greg Martin, the plant manager of 26 years. In came a new COO—a former consultant with an MBA and no manufacturing experience. His first move? Cut the R&D budget by 40%.

TriCraft's R&D team was small—just six engineers—but they were the ones helping clients solve tricky design problems, creating custom tooling, and keeping up with tighter aerospace specs. Cutting their budget didn't shut things down completely, but it did stall innovation. Projects got delayed. Client collaborations slowed. And slowly, customers began to notice.

Next came the property sale. Harding Tate sold the TriCraft facility to a real estate investment firm they were connected to, then leased it back. On paper, it looked like a smart move—cash came in from the sale. In practice,

TriCraft now had to pay monthly rent for the same building it used to own. It was a way to pull money out of the company without touching the operations—at least for now. But it added a new fixed cost. Want to expand or renovate? Now you needed the landlord's approval—and you were paying interest on cash you never really saw.

Then the maintenance cuts rolled in. TriCraft used to have strict preventative maintenance: every core machine got serviced monthly. It cost money, but surprise breakdowns cost more. That policy was tossed. The new COO introduced a quarterly review system that prioritized maintenance based on return on investment. In reality, it meant delaying service as long as possible.

This is where the cracks started to show. Machines took longer to warm up. Tooling errors cropped up more often. Minor problems—misaligned spindles, slipping belts—took longer to fix because parts weren't kept in stock anymore. Slowly, the line between smart savings and cutting corners began to blur.

Then came the people problem. In the first 18 months after the buyout, 15 of TriCraft's 80 machinists left. Most were senior workers. Some retired early, others moved to competitors or opened their own shops. Many were frustrated by the growing bureaucracy and what one veteran called "bean counters trying to run a foundry."

Replacing them was tough. Skilled machinists don't grow on trees. TriCraft had always trained people from within, but that took time. Harding Tate didn't want to wait. So, they turned to temp agencies and contractors. Those workers filled the spots, but not the experience gap.

Product quality started to dip. Not in big, obvious ways—but in small, important ones. A few parts didn't meet tight specs. Surface finishes weren't quite right. Internal defect rates rose. Clients who'd been loyal for years started asking for extra inspections. Some began shifting orders to competitors "just in case."

But from a financial point of view? Things looked great. By the end of year two, TriCraft had record EBITDA numbers. Costs were down. Headcount was lower. The company had squeezed more profit out of every dollar spent. It looked like a textbook success story—exactly the kind private equity firms like to showcase at conferences.

But walk the floor, and it felt different. Machines ran longer hours but broke down more. New hires needed more help but got less. Engineers were buried in spreadsheets instead of working with clients. Even long-time managers were quietly checking job listings during lunch.

One R&D engineer summed it up simply: "They took the soul out of the place. We used to solve problems. Now we just chase savings."

Harding Tate's plan was always short-term. In 2016, five years after buying TriCraft, they sold it to a larger aerospace conglomerate—also backed by private equity. They made a solid return. EBITDA was up. But the company itself? It wasn't the same.

TriCraft still exists. It still makes parts. It still employs people. But its place in the industry has changed. Where it once was a go-to partner for complex jobs, now it's just another vendor. Clients are cautious. Workers are less invested. The long-standing relationships that once held the business together have started to fray.

This isn't a story about fraud or bad intentions. It's a story about financial logic—applied without pause. The goal was never better machines or better parts. The goal was better returns. Every move—cutting R&D, scaling back maintenance, selling property, changing leadership—pushed toward that goal. And each move chipped away at what made TriCraft strong in the first place.

The people who pay that price aren't the investors. They're the workers who lose pride in their jobs, the clients who lose reliability, and the communities that lose steady employers. Private equity didn't invent short-term thinking in business—but it gave it a system, a formula, and a language that made it sound smart.

TriCraft is just one example, but it shows how fast a solid company can be hollowed out—not by failure, not by competitors, but by a model that values short-term returns over long-term strength.

Because here's the truth: you can't spreadsheet your way into better parts. That takes time, care, and reinvestment. When those things get replaced by financial targets and exit timelines, it's not just the company that suffers. It's the whole ecosystem around it—one piece at a time.

It would be nice—almost comforting—to blame what happened to TriCraft on a few greedy executives or one bad deal. That way, the problem would feel fixable: remove the villains, fix the outcome. But that's not how it works. The hard truth is, what happened to TriCraft isn't a fluke. It's the result of a system that not only allows this kind of thing—it encourages it. In some circles, it's even applauded.

The way our economy is set up today, it actually rewards decisions that hurt companies in the long run. At nearly every step—how companies are funded, how success is measured, how leaders get paid—the system leans heavily toward short-term profit instead of long-term health. These aren't just occasional missteps. They're baked into the rules.

Let's start with how deals are financed. If you're a private equity firm buying a company, chances are you're using debt, not equity, to pay for it. Why? Because it's cheaper, thanks to the tax code. In the U.S., interest on debt is tax-deductible, but dividends to shareholders are not. That gives debt financing a built-in advantage. The more you borrow, the less tax you pay. It's not just a loophole—it's a feature. That's why leveraged buyouts, like the one that reshaped TriCraft, are so appealing. They're not just possible— they're profitable.

This approach dates back to policies from the post–World War II era, when the goal was to drive investment and growth. But the world has changed, and now the same rules are used to boost returns through financial tricks, not by building stronger companies. The new strategy? Pile on debt, cut costs, show a temporary spike in earnings, and sell before things fall apart. The company pays the interest—and ends up stuck with the damage.

Then there's how we define success. In theory, companies exist to make things, create jobs, and solve problems. But in practice, many are judged by a few financial metrics. One of the most popular? EBITDA—earnings before interest, taxes, depreciation, and amortization. It's neat and tidy. It's also deeply flawed.

EBITDA ignores a lot of important stuff. It doesn't account for what a company spends to maintain equipment or invest in the future. It skips over whether workers are staying or burning out. But if your plan is to buy a company, boost EBITDA, and sell it in five years, then it's exactly what you want. You don't need the factory to run well for the next decade—just long enough to make the numbers look good on paper.

This isn't an accident. It's the way the system is designed.

Regulators haven't done much to stop it. There's still a strong belief, especially in some economic circles, that private markets will police themselves. If an investor runs a company into the ground, the thinking goes, the market will sort it out. But this ignores something big: when these deals go bad, it's usually not the investor who suffers. It's the company, and everyone who works there.

Harding Tate, the firm that bought TriCraft, made a solid profit. That TriCraft ended up weaker—less innovative, less stable—didn't matter. The firm had already exited.

They made their money. What happened after wasn't their problem. The system doesn't reward caretaking. It rewards cashing out.

Another trend feeding into this is who's leading companies. Increasingly, industrial firms are being run not by engineers or people who understand the nuts and bolts of the business, but by finance professionals. These are people who know how to read spreadsheets, not run shop floors. They can optimize a balance sheet but might not know the difference between TIG welding and MIG welding—or why either one matters.

That doesn't mean finance folks are bad at their jobs. But when leadership is disconnected from the core of the business, cost-cutting can start to look like a strategy. Leaders stop asking how to build better products and start asking how to make this quarter's numbers look a little better.

And the way we pay these leaders makes that worse. Executive bonuses are often tied to quick wins: cutting costs, bumping EBITDA, pushing the stock price up. There's rarely a reward for things like training workers, keeping clients for decades, or investing in better machines. Those things build lasting value—but they take time. And time is the one thing today's system doesn't want to wait for.

So financial engineering becomes more appealing than real engineering. It's faster. It shows up in quarterly reports. It pays off before the CEO moves on to their next job. Actual engineering—real innovation, durable progress—takes years to pay off. In a world obsessed with the next quarter, that kind of patience is seen as a risk.

This pressure isn't just on private equity firms. Public companies feel it too. Hedge funds often take aggressive stakes and demand immediate results. Boards get pushed to buy back stock instead of reinvesting profits. Wall Street loves certainty, not slow growth. Miss earnings by a penny, and your stock might tank—even if you're doing everything right for the long haul.

Here's a simple example: say you're choosing between building a new production line or outsourcing the work overseas. One takes money, training, and time. The other improves margins instantly. Guess which one usually wins.

As long as these core incentives stay in place, even the best policy ideas will struggle to make a dent. You can pass new laws to bring manufacturing home. You can roll out tax breaks and throw headlines around about rebuilding industry. But if the financial system still rewards stripping companies for parts instead of building them up, not much will really change.

A former manufacturing CEO said it best: "You can't run a world-class production facility on quarterly thinking. It's like trying to farm with a stopwatch."

So what could actually help?

There's no single fix, but there are some places to start.

First, the tax code. Right now, debt is favored over equity. That encourages loading companies with loans. Leveling the playing field would take away that advantage and reduce the appeal of risky, over-leveraged buyouts.

Second, accounting standards. EBITDA might be easy to track, but it doesn't tell the full story. What if companies had to report things like average machine age, backlogged maintenance, or how long their employees stay? That kind of info paints a clearer picture of a company's health.

Third, how we pay executives. If we want leaders to act like long-term stewards instead of short-term traders, we have to tie their pay to the long game. Bonuses could be based on product quality, employee retention, or how much is reinvested into the business—not just on whether the stock price went up.

Finally, we need to think about what we admire and reward. Right now, slashing costs and selling fast is seen as smart. That's what's taught in business schools. That's what gets written up in shareholder letters. But we almost never hear praise for the companies that quietly invest in their people, maintain their machines, and build for the future.

That cultural shift—what gets celebrated, what gets copied—is probably the toughest change of all. But without it, the old playbook will keep winning. And companies like TriCraft will keep losing.

TriCraft didn't fall apart all at once. It faded—cut by cut, deal by deal. Each decision seemed logical. Each step made sense on paper. But slowly, those decisions drained away what made the company strong: its people, its skills, and the steady rhythm of work done with care.

This isn't just about one company. It's about whether we still know how to build things that last. Real strength—whether in business, the economy, or the country—doesn't come from spreadsheets. It comes from hands-on work, long-term thinking, and the kind of patience that builds something worth keeping.

As long as the system rewards tearing things down over building them up, we'll keep getting more of the same. And the foundation we're standing on will only get weaker.

Jeff Leimbach

Chapter 4: The True Cost Ledger

When Wall Street talks about cost, it almost always means dollars. Everything gets boiled down to earnings reports, margins, and shareholder returns. A few cents shaved off production costs? That's a reason to celebrate. A slight bump in profits? Time to hand out bonuses. But what if the real price of doing business doesn't show up in those numbers? What if the most serious damage takes years to reveal itself—not on a spreadsheet, but in hollowed-out towns, weakened industries, and a country that can't make its own essentials?

For the past 40 years, we've been playing by a narrow set of rules—rules that miss the bigger picture. We became obsessed with efficiency, but never stopped to ask: efficient for whom? And what are we giving up in return?

Take printed circuit boards (PCBs), for example. These aren't flashy, but they're inside almost everything—phones, cars, even missiles. Back in the 1990s, the U.S. was a major player in PCB manufacturing. But by 2023, over 90% of PCBs came from Asia, mostly China. Why? Because it was cheaper. That shift saved companies money—but also left the U.S. dangerously dependent on others for something critical to modern technology. That cost didn't show up in the budget. It never does.

This isn't just about national security—though that's a big part of it. It's about the way we've let short-term thinking steer our entire economy. Decisions that look smart in a quarterly report can be a disaster when you zoom out. When a factory in the U.S. closes because another one overseas can do the same job a bit cheaper, it's not just a business move. It's a loss of skills, experience, and community strength. And that gamble—that global shipping will always be smooth, that trade relations will stay friendly—looked fine until COVID hit. Then we couldn't even get basic medical gear without scrambling.

And yet, we called this system "efficient." But that kind of lean, just-in-time supply chain only works when everything else is perfect—stable politics, cheap fuel, no unexpected shocks. The minute something breaks, it all comes crashing down. What we called optimized was actually fragile.

And the hidden costs? They're everywhere. When a plant in Pennsylvania that made aircraft-grade aluminum shuts down, it's not just jobs that disappear. The whole town changes. Tax money dries up. Schools lose funding. Small businesses close—diners, repair shops, hardware stores. Even the local newspaper might vanish. That factory wasn't just a workplace—it was the heart of the community.

What takes its place? Usually nothing. Or maybe a warehouse filled with products made in the very country that undercut the old factory. The town goes from being a place that builds things to a place that just moves boxes.

And none of that shows up when a procurement officer compares bids. All they see is that one supplier is 15% cheaper. That's it. No checkbox for risk if trade routes go down. No calculation for what happens if the domestic industry fades away. No way to account for laid-off workers, shuttered training programs, or kids who'll never learn a skilled trade.

Economists have a term for this: "externalities"—costs or benefits that fall on people outside the transaction. But try convincing a CFO that the ripple effects of closing a plastics plant in Ohio should show up on their balance sheet. That's like asking a shark to think about the feelings of the fish. The system just isn't built that way.

Still, these costs are real. They're not just theoretical. In the early days of the pandemic, we couldn't get enough N95 masks because we didn't make enough of them here anymore. Even after the government stepped in, it took time to catch up. Why? Because the companies that used to know how to do it had shut down or moved on. Starting that engine back up was like replanting an entire forest—slow, costly, and full of setbacks.

We talk about innovation like it's something that happens in white coats and pitch decks. But real innovation relies on people who know how to make things. Without factories, engineers get disconnected from production. Ideas stay stuck in notebooks because there's no one left to bring them to life. And over time, those bold ideas just stop coming.

Look at the original iPhone. It wasn't just about design—it worked because engineers and manufacturers worked hand in hand. That kind of collaboration is harder when the people designing a product are in California and the people building it are 7,000 miles away in China. Distance weakens teamwork. Eventually, it weakens ability.

Offshoring alone isn't the villain here. The deeper problem is how companies define success. For too many, it's all about short-term gain. Cut research spending. Lay off skilled workers. Move operations to cheaper countries. Squeeze every last cent out of vendors. Then use the savings to buy back stock and pump up earnings per share. It's all perfectly legal—and slowly killing the system from the inside.

What's missing is a sense of long-term strategy. A strong industrial base isn't just a way to make money—it's a kind of safety net for the whole country. It helps us handle surprises, keeps communities alive, and powers new ideas. Without it, we don't just lose jobs—we lose our independence. We end up at the mercy of countries that may not have our best interests at heart.

And here's the strange part: we already know this. After World War II, the U.S. invested heavily in its industrial base—not just to win the war, but to be ready for the future. We poured money into research, training, infrastructure, and domestic production. The payoff was huge—economic growth, world-leading technology, strong communities, and a middle class that was the envy of the world.

We've done it before. We can do it again. But not if we keep measuring success with the same old tools. Not if the only thing that matters is cutting costs, instead of building something that lasts. Not if we keep mistaking the bottom line for the whole story.

To bring back real industrial strength, we have to start counting differently. We need new ways to measure success—ones that include things like supply chain strength, not just cost savings. Metrics that value resilience, not just return on investment. Accounting that takes into account what we lose when we let vital industries fade away.

In other words, we need to see the full picture. Not just the profit—but the price we're paying.

If you want to kill innovation, you don't need to ban science or destroy factories. Just put the whole thing in the hands of a spreadsheet.

For decades, American manufacturing grew through a mix of curiosity, skill, and patience. Innovation was slow, sometimes painfully so—but it moved forward. It came from engineers tweaking designs on the shop floor, suppliers testing new materials, and R&D teams with the freedom to think in years, not quarters. It wasn't flashy, but it was real. Progress came from constant feedback, trial and error, and a strong connection between the people who designed things and the people who built them.

Then came a different kind of engineer.

Not the kind with safety goggles and torque wrenches. These were financial engineers—in suits, working in private equity firms, investment banks, and the upper floors of corporate headquarters. Their tools weren't CAD programs or machine presses. They used leverage, arbitrage, and stock buybacks. Their genius wasn't in fixing technical problems. It was in squeezing profits, dressing up balance sheets, and making returns look good.

One of their favorite moves? Cutting costs in all the wrong places—especially the ones that made innovation possible.

Take a former aerospace supplier in Wichita, Kansas. For years, it had quietly built parts for some of the most advanced aircraft in the world. It wasn't a big name, but it had a talented group of engineers and a strong R&D team working on something important: a new composite material that was lighter than aluminum and could handle extreme heat. This wasn't science fiction. It was a real, doable idea that could have made planes more efficient and cut down emissions.

Then a private equity firm bought the company.

They called it "streamlining." What it really meant was slashing R&D, cutting jobs, and boosting short-term profits for a future sale. Within months, the research team was gutted, engineers let go, and the composite project shelved. Years of work—gone. A breakthrough that might have changed the industry was quietly buried.

No press coverage. No public backlash. Just another "business decision."

And this kind of thing wasn't rare.

In the medical device world, a similar story played out. A mid-sized company in the Midwest had made a name for itself by designing and building high-quality implantable devices. What set them apart was their in-house approach—they handled design, prototyping, and manufacturing themselves. That meant engineers, machinists, and even clinical advisors worked side by side. They could spot problems early and move fast.

Then the investors came knocking. Pressured to hit tough earnings targets, the company looked for quick savings. Outsourcing seemed like a smart move. Cheaper parts made overseas meant better margins. On paper, it worked. Profits went up. The stock rose. Executives got applause for "smart cost management."

But inside, things were falling apart.

The knowledge that had once lived inside the company—details about materials, tolerances, and how devices interacted with the body—started disappearing. Engineers left. Skilled workers were reassigned or let go. Collaboration faded. Eventually, innovation slowed—not because they stopped trying, but because the system that once made it possible had been hollowed out.

You can't outsource curiosity. And you can't schedule creativity to fit your quarterly earnings call.

The big picture is just as worrying. In 1980, U.S. manufacturers spent around 5.5% of their revenue on R&D. By 2022, that number had dropped to about 2.3%. Some industries—like pharma—kept investing. But in many areas of traditional manufacturing, the decline was sharp.

And the effects showed. Between 1980 and 2020, the average time between new product generations got longer in many sectors. Instead of speeding up, companies were slowing down. Fewer big breakthroughs. Longer waits between upgrades. Innovation started to mean tiny changes instead of big leaps.

Patent numbers tell the same story. Total patent filings went up—thanks mostly to growth in software and biotech—but manufacturing-related patents leveled off. And even when patents were filed, their impact— measured by how often they were cited or actually used—dropped. We were filing more, but building less.

Some say that's just maturity. Maybe we picked all the easy wins. But that's a neat excuse, especially for those profiting from the current system. The harder truth? We drained the lifeblood from innovation on purpose.

Why? Because the way we measured success stopped valuing it.

To a CEO trying to hit next quarter's earnings, R&D is just another cost. Training workers? Too expensive. Building relationships with suppliers? Doesn't move the stock. These things don't pay off quickly, so they're often the first to go. It's like running a farm and cutting back on seeds and fertilizer to save money. Sure, you'll lower costs—for a while. But don't be surprised when your crops stop growing.

There's also the loss of know-how—not just people leaving, but whole systems of knowledge breaking down. Back when American industry was at its peak, innovation didn't happen in a vacuum. It came from tight-knit networks—skilled workers, engineers, and suppliers working closely together. A line worker might notice a small flaw. A machinist might invent a faster way to cut a part. A supplier might come up with a new alloy. These weren't headline-grabbing discoveries, but they added up. They were the quiet engine behind real progress.

When companies sent production overseas or farmed it out to the cheapest bidder, those networks broke. The casual hallway conversations, the spontaneous problem-solving, the hands-on collaboration—all of it vanished. What took its place was cold and disconnected: CAD files emailed to unknown contractors, updates sent by spreadsheet, and a growing gap between those who designed and those who built.

Innovation didn't stop. It just got harder. Slower. Riskier.

And in fast-moving fields like semiconductors, aerospace, and clean energy, delays are deadly. If your rival can go through five design rounds while you're still waiting for your first prototype to ship back from across the ocean, you've already lost.

Some companies tried to push back. They reinvested in local talent, rebuilt supplier relationships, and fought to protect their engineering teams. But they were fighting against a strong current. Investors wanted quick returns. Activist shareholders wanted higher margins. And executive bonuses were tied to quarterly numbers. Long-term thinking rarely won.

Even when the math supported innovation, it didn't always matter. There's a story about a robotics company that built a new modular system for factory automation— something that could save huge amounts of time and money. The tech worked. The numbers checked out. But the board, pressured by private equity owners, refused to fund it. Too much capital spending. Too much risk. So the project sat on the shelf.

Years later, a German competitor launched a similar system—and took over a huge share of the market. The American firm, now on its third set of owners, had faded into obscurity.

That's the real damage of financial extraction: it doesn't just cut costs. It cuts off the future.

We like to say that the market rewards innovation, that capitalism lifts up the best ideas. But that only works when the incentives line up. When money is patient. When risk is allowed. When we value building over flipping.

Instead, we've created a system where anything that doesn't pay off immediately is seen as a waste. That's not just a problem—it's a flaw in the design. One we built into the system ourselves.

If we want to bring American manufacturing back—not just the jobs, but the leadership—we have to rebuild what made it strong in the first place. That means putting real money and real time into R&D. It means supporting people and processes, not just profits. It means rebuilding supplier networks where experimentation can thrive. And it means giving teams the space to work on big ideas, even if they take years to develop.

Maybe most of all, it means changing who we cheer for. Are we rewarding the people who improve how things are made—or just the ones who hit the right numbers?

Because if all we care about is squeezing costs, we'll keep squeezing out the very things that made us great. But if we care about lasting progress—about doing hard, meaningful work—we'll have to get comfortable with the messy, expensive, and slow path of real innovation. And that's the one path worth taking.

For most of the last hundred years, Gross Domestic Product was the scoreboard. If GDP was going up, things were good—or so we thought. Politicians made it their rallying cry, economists tracked it obsessively, and Wall Street treated it like gospel. A higher number meant progress, prosperity, and proof that the system was working.

But somewhere along the line, that number stopped telling the full story.

GDP rises when a hedge fund buys a factory and lays off 800 workers—because profits go up. It rises when a hospital is taken over by private equity and slashes services while hiking prices—because revenue grows. It even rises after a hurricane when we rebuild. GDP doesn't ask whether what's happening is good or bad for people. It just tracks motion. Any motion. More money moving through the system? Great. Whether that movement builds or breaks—doesn't matter.

Yet we still treat it as the gold standard for national prosperity. That's like judging someone's health just by their weight. You might be looking at an athlete—or someone dangerously ill. Same number, completely different meaning.

Our economy has been "gaining weight" for decades, but in many ways, it's been wasting away on the inside. While GDP and stock prices have soared, we've lost real productive power, seen communities unravel, and given up control over key parts of our supply chain. You can't build a strong nation by flipping assets and trading paper. At some point, you have to make things. And right now, we're not even measuring the things that matter.

If we want to rebuild what's been lost, we first need to change how we measure success.

This isn't about throwing out GDP or turning our backs on markets. It's about broadening the view. We need more tools on the dashboard—metrics that show us strength, stability, and long-term potential, not just short-term profits. We need a new kind of ledger. One that counts what really counts.

Let's start with something called the Manufacturing Vulnerability Index (MVI). You probably haven't heard of it yet, but it could end up being one of the most important numbers we track. MVI doesn't just show how much we make—it shows how easily that could fall apart. It asks: Where are we overly dependent on other countries? How concentrated is our supply chain? How fast could we ramp up production at home if we had to? It's not just about capability—it's about control.

Take semiconductors. MVI analysis reveals how dangerously exposed the U.S. is—not just in making the chips themselves, but in the machines, chemicals, and materials that go into them. A single disruption in Taiwan or South Korea could ripple through our entire economy. The same goes for aerospace materials, rare earths, and even basic pharmaceutical ingredients. MVI doesn't just tell us there's a problem. It shows how deep it goes and where we're most vulnerable.

But it's not enough to know where we're weak. We also need to understand where we're strong—and where we could be stronger.

That's where Community Resilience Scores come in. This isn't just feel-good fluff. It's a grounded look at how well a local economy can take a hit and keep going. It measures things like how many kinds of jobs exist, how solid the public services are, whether there's vocational training available, and how stable local tax revenues are. Basically, is this town or city built to last?

Picture two towns, each with a factory. In one, the factory is the only major employer, making a part for products that are mostly made overseas. In the other, there are several midsize manufacturers, strong local training programs, and a college working closely with businesses to develop talent. When a global supply chain problem hits, which town recovers faster? The answer's obvious. But GDP wouldn't see the difference. In fact, it might even treat a factory closing as a win if it boosts corporate earnings.

Tracking resilience over time helps spot which regions are on solid ground and which are quietly falling apart. More importantly, it gives us a way to reward the places doing the hard work to build lasting, adaptive local economies—not just chasing the next flashy deal.

Then there's the Innovation Sustainability Index. It might be a mouthful, but it matters.

Innovation isn't just about coming up with the next big idea. It's about having the systems, people, and investments in place to keep those ideas coming. This index looks at things like long-term R&D spending, the health of talent pipelines, capital reinvestment, patent quality, and partnerships between schools and industry. If the MVI shows where we're at risk, and the resilience score shows how we're holding up, this index shows where we're headed. It's like checking the gas tank before a road trip. Are we fueling our future—or coasting on fumes?

Some places are already trying parts of this approach. In Massachusetts, there's a program linking technical high schools with manufacturers, tracking not just how many kids graduate but how many get good jobs. In Ohio, regional manufacturing hubs are using new metrics that tie public funding to job quality—not just how many people get hired, but how well those jobs support families. These are small steps, but they point in the right direction.

We've spent so long treating the economy like a stock chart that we've forgotten it's really made up of people, places, and relationships. Offshoring didn't just cost jobs. It pulled apart entire ecosystems—shop-floor knowledge, community pride, tax bases that funded schools and hospitals. The human infrastructure behind the numbers.

None of that shows up in GDP. But you can see it in other places: higher suicide rates, struggling small towns, crowded food banks, and falling life expectancy. Once we stopped counting those things, we stopped paying attention. And when no one's watching, things break.

Fixing this won't be easy. It's not just about tweaking a few policies or negotiating better trade deals. It's about changing what we value—and how we track progress.

We need to reward patience over quick profits. That could mean changing executive pay so bonuses are tied to improvements in resilience or domestic capacity—not just the stock price. It could mean offering tax breaks to companies that reinvest in their workers and equipment. It could mean setting clear goals for community economic health, so states and cities compete on long-term success—not just snagging the next big factory.

And it has to mean holding Wall Street to a new standard. If a private equity firm guts a manufacturer to boost short-term gains, that shouldn't be called "efficiency." It's a strategic risk, and it should be treated as such. Right now, markets price risk as if national fragility doesn't matter. That has to change.

Most of all, we need to stop treating growth as the only thing that matters.

Growth isn't good if it comes from hollowing out what made us strong in the first place. Moving a factory from Ohio to Vietnam might lift corporate profits—but it makes us weaker, less secure, and more dependent. Cheap products aren't a win if they cost us our ability to stand on our own two feet.

Capitalism still has a role to play—but it has to be capitalism with memory. The kind that remembers what made America strong in the first place: connection to place, to people, and to purpose.

Real prosperity in the years ahead won't come from chasing the next quarter's numbers. It'll come from building something deeper. An economy that can take a punch and keep moving. One that doesn't fall apart when a ship gets stuck in a canal or a foreign government shifts its policy. One that grows not just wide—but with roots.

That means tracking new things. Lifting up new kinds of leadership. Making new kinds of choices.

And recognizing that the real loss isn't just in what we've stopped making—it's in who we've stopped investing in.

Getting it back won't be easy. But it starts with seeing the whole picture.

And finally, deciding it's time to count what really matters.

Jeff Leimbach

Chapter 5: The Ghost Factory – Middle America's Lost Industrial Commons

The Factory Town That Built America
You won't find Millcrest, Ohio, in many history books. It's not the birthplace of a president or the site of any famous battle. But if you want to know how America once built a middle class—not in theory, but in real, everyday life—Millcrest is where you start.

Take a drive down what used to be Main Avenue. The buildings are still there—red brick, windows cracked or boarded up, paint peeling off like old wallpaper. A line of rusted railroad tracks runs along the edge of town, once busy hauling out gearboxes and engine parts bound for Detroit, Milwaukee, and all over the country. In the middle of it all sits what's left of the factory that kept this place alive for generations.

That factory, Millcrest Tool & Die, was the town's lifeblood. At its peak in the late '70s, it employed more than 3,200 people. The work wasn't glamorous, but it was honest, skilled, and paid well. An 18-year-old fresh out of high school could walk in, get trained, and earn enough to buy a home, raise a family, and retire comfortably. You didn't need a polished résumé—just a friend or family member already on the floor. Around here, people didn't ask, "What do you do?" They asked, "What shift you working?"

It might sound like a dream today, but for many years, it was reality. In the cafeteria, union workers sat next to supervisors. On Saturdays, even the managers came out to mow the Little League field. Nobody had yachts, but nobody was scraping by either. As Bill Dugan, a retired machinist, put it, "We all pulled from the same rope. We had skin in the game, and the game was ours."

Millcrest was what economists now call an "industrial commons"—a tight-knit mix of skills, suppliers, shops, training centers, and old-school knowledge that, together, made world-class manufacturing possible. It wasn't just the big factory. It was the ten little businesses nearby that made fasteners, lubricants, conveyor belts, and spare parts. It was the local tech college that taught welding and toolmaking. It was the small machine shop where a guy named Leon could eyeball a busted gear and say, "Yeah, I can get you one of those by Tuesday."

The town was like an ecosystem. Sure, the factory was the tallest tree, but everything else—the soil, the roots, the bees, the smaller plants—kept it all alive. Lose the tree, and it's not just the shade that goes. The whole system starts to fall apart.

And here's the thing: Millcrest wasn't some outlier. It was one dot on a huge map of towns across the Midwest and beyond. Fort Wayne. Toledo. Janesville. Erie. Every one of them had a factory at the center and a web of small businesses and workers built around it. These weren't just places where people clocked in and out—they were communities shaped by what they made.

There's a story folks in Millcrest still like to tell, even if it's tinged with nostalgia now. In 1981, a high school junior named Mike Novak skipped school one Friday to help his dad at the plant. His dad had hurt his back lifting a heavy casting, so Mike stepped in to run the lathe. He worked through the weekend—26 hours total—and left with a paycheck for $360. That was real money back then. When he brought it home, his mom cried. Not because he skipped school, but because she knew he was going to be okay.

By the time Mike graduated, the plant had offered him a full-time job. He never even thought about college. "Why would I?" he said when I visited him last year. "By 22, I was making more than my high school principal."

That kind of steady, hands-on work gave people a sense of security and belonging. They weren't chasing side gigs or updating LinkedIn profiles. They were building things—real things—and taking pride in doing it right. Some might call it old-fashioned now, but it was built on a simple promise: Show up, learn the trade, do your best, and there's a place for you.

And it wasn't just the workers who benefited. The whole town did. The local government had money to fix roads and fund music and science programs in schools. Diners stayed busy. Kids could play safely in the streets. The community didn't just live here—it worked together, in every sense of the word.

The strength of Millcrest wasn't just one big factory. It was how the whole place worked like a machine. Teachers taught the children of toolmakers. Local banks offered loans based on steady plant paychecks. Churches ran bake sales that sold out in an hour. Even the Fourth of July parade had floats sponsored by different departments in the plant. One banner read, "CNC Machinists—Proud to Be Union Made."

People took pride in their work—serious pride. The parts they made powered transatlantic ships and shaped the chrome on Ford Mustangs. And when they saw those parts out in the world, it was like spotting their signature out there in the metal. Not flashy, not loud—but strong, dependable, and built to last.

Even more than the pay or the skills, what mattered most was the sense that building real things—heavy, useful, important things—meant something. There was a kind of quiet honor in being part of the engine that kept the country moving. As one foreman put it, "We're not flashy. But we built the damn country."

That pride ran deep. Every morning at 7 a.m., when the factory bell rang, it was like a town-wide alarm clock. Lights flicked on. Coffee brewed. People headed off to jobs they knew mattered. There was a rhythm to life here, a sense of purpose that came from seeing something through, start to finish, and knowing you helped make it real.

That rhythm kept the town moving for almost a hundred years. Millcrest Tool & Die made it through wars, recessions, buyouts, and strikes. No matter what came, it always found a way to bounce back.

What folks didn't see coming—at least not clearly, not soon enough—was that the factory wasn't just at risk from market dips or foreign competition. It was at risk from something more distant, more invisible. From decisions made in far-off boardrooms, by people who never set foot in Millcrest, and never heard that factory bell ring. To them, this town wasn't a community—it was a number on a spreadsheet.

That part of the story—when things started to fall apart—comes later. But before you can understand what was lost, you have to see what was really there.

Millcrest was more than just a place that made parts. It was a place that made a way of life. For decades, it wasn't a cautionary tale. It was a model. A promise. A future that, for a while, actually worked.

The warning signs didn't show up all at once. To most folks in Millcrest, everything at Titan Machine Works still looked steady well into the 1980s. Sure, there were a few whispers—management changes, some unfamiliar guys in suits poking around with clipboards—but nothing that raised real concern. The factory had been through tough times before. It had weathered the Vietnam draft, the oil crisis, even a strike in '72 that almost turned into a bonfire in the parking lot. People counted on Titan. Or maybe they just couldn't picture life without it.

Then came the buyout.

In 1988, Titan was sold to a private equity firm out of Chicago called Sterling Partners—a name that sounded more like a law office than anything to do with machining or metal. The local newspaper ran a hopeful article with phrases like "strategic alignment" and "growth opportunities." The mayor showed up for a ribbon-cutting, there were handshakes and speeches, and everyone smiled for the cameras. But behind all that, something had started to shift.

At first, it was quiet. A few department heads retired—not loudly, just quietly faded out. Some had been pushed; others saw what was coming and decided to leave on their own. A new org chart made its way around, though hardly anyone understood it. Somehow, engineers were now reporting to finance.

Then the new plant manager arrived.

Ron Heffley, who had worked his way up from the shop floor since 1953 and knew every machine like a friend, was replaced by a young executive with slick shoes and an MBA. His name was Alan Breckinridge. He spoke in buzzwords, smiled too much, and clearly didn't get the place. He didn't show up to the Friday night fish fry at St. Luke's. Didn't seem to understand why people stayed after their shifts to help someone finish a job. To him, the factory wasn't a legacy or a community—it was a spreadsheet with numbers to trim.

By 1990, the trimming began.

IT was the first to go. The old system— homegrown by a couple of smart guys who had once run it from a trailer out back—was scrapped. In its place came a sleek, outsourced platform from New Jersey. It looked good on paper, but nobody knew how to use it. Orders got lost. Tools went missing. Schedules turned into guesswork. Engineers grumbled. Machinists swore. One supervisor joked, "We used to know where the wrench was—now it's lost in the cloud."

Next came R&D.

Titan had always prided itself on careful, quiet innovation. They didn't chase patents for headlines. They improved things— stronger parts, tighter fits, better alloys. But the new CFO didn't see the value. R&D's budget got slashed by nearly 40 percent. "Too speculative," he said. "Not aligned with our current revenue goals." The team that once designed a gear tooth used by Navy submarines was now told to focus on filling out forms and finding ways to cut costs.

But the layoffs were what really shook Millcrest.

They hit on a Thursday. A third of the engineering team—people who had spent their whole careers at Titan—were suddenly gone. Some packed up boxes. Some got calls at home. The official word was "operational streamlining." A phrase so vague it only made people feel worse.

"It was like chopping down a tree at the roots," said Linda Koepke, who ran HR at the time. "These weren't just employees. They helped build this place. Shape it. You can't cut people like that and think everything stays the same."

But that was the plan. Things weren't staying the same.

Outside the plant, the ripple effects started. Local suppliers—some family businesses that had served Titan for generations—began getting strange phone calls from Titan's new procurement team. No more back-and-forth about how to tweak a part or speed up production. Now it was just: "Can you match this quote?"

And the quote? Always from overseas. China, mostly. Sometimes Malaysia. It didn't matter that the part was complicated, or that shipping took weeks, or that the specs would probably need adjusting. All that mattered was the price on the screen.

Leon Gerber, who owned Gerber Precision Tools just north of town, remembers the day everything changed. "They sent over this tricky little bearing housing we'd made for them for years," he said. "They didn't ask if we could speed it up or improve the design. They just said, 'Here's a quote from China. Can you beat it?'" He shook his head. "They didn't want partners anymore. Just bidders."

The relationships disappeared. Meetings with vendors used to be held over coffee in the breakroom, with drawings sketched on napkins. Now, everything was uploaded to a portal. Bids were entered into dashboards. Calls stopped coming. Weeks would go by without a word.

Even inside the factory, things felt different. The lightness, the teamwork—it faded. People moved with their heads down. When a machine broke, no one gathered around to fix it together. They just looked around, hoping they wouldn't be blamed. Everyone was on edge. Everyone felt replaceable.

And the changes just kept rolling in.

In 1991, Titan sold its land and buildings in a sale-leaseback deal. Property that had been paid off over decades was now owned by a real estate firm. Titan rented its own space. "It was like selling your house and moving into the basement," said Mike Novak, a longtime production supervisor. "We built this place. And now we were tenants."

The money from the sale didn't go into better tools or safety upgrades. It went to pay off the debt—the same debt created by the buyout. Titan, once nearly debt-free, was now deep in the red. Interest payments grew each quarter, eating up cash that used to go toward raises, training, or new machines.

The machines suffered. Maintenance schedules got stretched thin. Some replacement parts were skipped. The older, more accurate mills were slowly shut down.

When they were replaced, it was with cheap machines that couldn't hold tight specs. Defects started to creep in. Orders ran late. Customers weren't happy.

But if you sat in on the quarterly meetings, you'd never know. The execs wore big smiles and showed graphs heading up and to the right. "EBITDA growth looks strong," they said. "Margins are improving." Not a word about broken drills or missed deadlines.

For folks in Millcrest, it all felt backward.

"You could tell they were making money," said Bill Dugan, who came out of retirement to work part-time. "But we weren't making good parts anymore. It was like they'd figured out how to squeeze money out of the factory without actually running it right. That's when I knew something was wrong."

And there was a word for it. Extraction.

Titan wasn't being run to build machines or serve customers. It was being stripped—turned into a money source for people who didn't care about machining, or the workers, or even the long-term health of the company. The factory wasn't a place to build. It was something to bleed dry.

The people in charge didn't need to know how to cut steel or read a tolerance sheet. They just needed to know how to move money around, fast and quietly. The value wasn't in the factory, the workers, or the product. It was in how much they could pull out before the whole thing fell apart.

And Millcrest wasn't alone. This was happening in Toledo. In South Bend. In Muncie. All over the Midwest, places that used to make things were being quietly gutted—not by failure, but on purpose.

"I used to think we were the backbone of the country," said Linda Koepke. "But a backbone only works if you stand tall. We were bending ourselves in circles just to hit targets made by people who'd never stepped foot in a machine shop."

And while the profits went up on paper, a way of life was coming undone.

The high school cut its shop program. The local college shut down its tool-and-die course. Leon had to lay off two of his five workers. The diner near the plant stopped serving lunch—just mornings now. The Little League field didn't get mowed one summer because no one had time, or maybe they just didn't have the heart.

A town built around hard work and skill was becoming a place where people waited. Waited for jobs to come back. Waited for calls. Waited for hope.

But it never came. Not from Chicago. Not from Wall Street. Not from anywhere.

For generations, Millcrest ran on the belief that if you worked hard, did good work, and stood by your neighbors, you had a place. You didn't have to get rich. You just had to count for something.

Now, for the first time, people weren't sure they did.

The last shift at Titan ended on a gray Tuesday in 2003. No farewell speeches, no sendoff—just a few folks cleaning out lockers, dropping off badges, and heading out to a half-empty parking lot. One machinist forgot his lunchbox. Someone scrawled "Good luck" on the break room whiteboard. After more than sixty years, the machines stopped. The thud of presses, the grind of metal, the constant hum that had filled the valley for generations—gone. Silence settled in.

But not everyone was ready to let go.

About six months later, an old garage at the edge of town started buzzing again. The sign out front said "Harvey's Repair & Fabrication," hand-painted in faded red. Inside, surrounded by aging drill presses and a welder older than he was, stood Harvey Molina.

Harvey had worked at Titan for 28 years. He started back in 1975, when you still punched in with a metal timecard and every foreman had a pencil tucked behind his ear. When the layoffs came, he hung on as long as he could—took night shifts, learned to run the new CNC machines, even supervised a mostly-idle line. When the plant finally closed, he walked away with a box of tools, two bad vertebrae, and a severance check that barely covered the mortgage.

He could've retired. He was almost 60. But Harvey wasn't wired for sitting still.

"I still had grease under my nails," he said. "Didn't know what else to do."

So he rented a drafty garage near home and got back to work. Tractors. Old bikes. The occasional busted jack. Word spread fast. Farmers liked that he charged fair prices. Truckers liked that he could machine a missing part instead of replacing a whole system. Some days he'd work twelve hours straight with nothing but a thermos of coffee and a country station playing on a dusty radio.

Then came Malik—with a broken go-kart axle and a lot of questions.

Seventeen, smart, but barely staying afloat in school. His dad had been in and out of prison, his mom worked double shifts, and the high school shop class had been cut years ago. He'd found the kart at a yard sale and wanted to fix it. He just didn't know how.

"I thought he wanted a quote," Harvey said. "But he asked if he could stay and watch me work."

So Harvey let him. Showed him how to measure runout on the lathe, how to stay safe around the spinning parts, how to read a weld's grain. Malik came back the next Saturday. Then the next. Then he brought a friend. Then another.

Within a year, Harvey had a rotating crew of teens showing up every weekend—learning how to bend metal, run a drill press, and why torque specs matter.

He didn't charge a dime. "I ain't running a school," he'd say. "Just passing it on."

That phrase—passing it on—meant more than Harvey let on. Because to him, machining wasn't just work. It was a way of thinking. Of solving real problems with your hands and your mind. Of choosing precision over shortcuts, pride over speed. And it was disappearing.

"They don't teach this stuff anymore," he said. "These kids grow up tapping on screens, not tapping threads."

But in Harvey's garage, the lights stayed on. The smell of oil and hot steel still hung in the air. The skills didn't vanish—they just found new hands.

Meanwhile, two miles across town, in a small one-story house under a row of old sugar maples, someone else was keeping history alive in her own way.

Marta Jensen, now in her seventies, used to be a lead design engineer at Titan. She'd started in the mid-1960s, one of the very few women on the technical side of the floor. Her specialty? Thermal tolerances—how to make parts that could take intense heat without warping. Submarine valves, jet parts, reactor components—she'd worked on them all.

When the plant started laying people off, Marta pushed back. Quietly, but firmly. She wrote memos. Spoke up in meetings. Tried to make the case that true innovation needs steady hands, not constant cuts. Eventually, they let her go. But she didn't leave empty-handed. She walked out with boxes of technical drawings, design guides, and stacks of engineering notebooks that no one else wanted.

"They were gonna trash them," she said. "Fifty years of work. All those drafts, notes, calculations—just gone. I couldn't let that happen."

So she took them home. Filled the garage, then the spare bedroom. Bought a secondhand scanner online and started digitizing everything. Nights, weekends—even on holidays—she'd be at her desk, uploading decades of Titan's design knowledge.

Why?

"Because if we forget how we did it, we won't be able to do it again."

Marta wasn't holding on out of nostalgia. She was holding on because she believed it mattered. Someday, she figured, America would need to make real things again—not just assemble, but actually design, machine, and build from scratch. And when that time came, someone would need the old knowledge.

So she labeled every file. Cross-referenced every binder. Even made a website. It's clunky, sure—but it works. A few young engineers stumbled on it, reached out, and were shocked to find technical specs from the 1970s still available.

"I told them: metal doesn't forget," Marta said with a smile. "You just have to know what to ask."

To some, her project might seem strange or sentimental. But to others, it's something more. A small, stubborn flame still burning. She never made speeches or wrote think-pieces. But in her own way, she kept the old line alive.

Just a few blocks from where Titan's front gate once stood—now just cracked pavement and windblown weeds—there's a different kind of buzz coming from the old conference wing. Most of the factory still sits empty, but that one wing has been cleaned up and brought back to life. Inside is the office of Councilwoman Renee Calhoon.

Renee grew up right in Millcrest. Her dad ran a plating shop. Her mom pulled night shifts at the hospital. After college, where she studied urban planning, she came back home, determined not just to remember what used to be—but to help shape what could be.

She ran for city council in 2018 on a platform nobody expected: rebuilding the industrial base. Not with tax breaks for big-box stores, but with real investment in modern manufacturing—advanced materials, 3D printing, robotics. She called it "next-gen grit."

At first, people didn't take her seriously. Then she rolled out a plan: an advanced manufacturing incubator, funded by the state, built right on the old Titan site. She argued that the structure was still solid, the foundations strong. The only thing missing? Opportunity.

"People kept asking, 'Why here?'" Renee said. "And I told them, 'Because here is where we already know how to build. We just need to believe it again.'"

She faced pushback. Some locals laughed it off. Others said it would never work. But Renee kept showing up. She met with state reps. Took high school students on field trips to tech factories. Won one grant, then another. She brought in a community college, an automation startup, even a defense contractor looking for specialty parts.

And bit by bit, things changed. The empty wing filled with laptops and blueprints. Then interns. Then techs. Machines arrived—not the huge, roaring beasts of the old days, but smaller, faster, smarter. Still loud in their own way.

It's not a full comeback—not yet. But it's a start.

"We're not trying to rebuild the past," Renee said. "We're building for what's next. And that starts with people. With skills. With places to learn and build. You can't ship that in."

The project's still delicate. Funding is always a fight. Politics shift. But Renee keeps going. She holds town halls. She listens. She plans. She pushes.

And when you ask her why, she doesn't talk about numbers or jobs reports. She talks about meaning.

"Work should mean something," she said. "It should build you up, not break you down. That's what I want for Millcrest."

There's no magic fix. The factory won't fill up overnight. The old suppliers are long gone. The know-how that took generations to build won't return in one training session.

But in a little garage, a quiet home archive, and a repurposed office wing, the sparks are still alive. People are still trying. Still holding the torch.

Because rebuilding isn't just about policies or politics. It's about remembering. Teaching. Imagining what's possible.

It's about taking what worked—and making it work again, in a new way.

Harvey's garage still smells like cutting oil and sawdust. Marta's spare bedroom glows with the light of a scanner. Renee's office wall holds a photo of her dad's shop—framed in brushed steel.

They're not preserving a museum. They're building a future.

And in their quiet persistence, there's hope. Not loud. Not flashy.

But real.

The kind you can build on.

Chapter 6: The Knowledge Problem

In manufacturing, there's a kind of knowledge you won't find in spreadsheets or training manuals. It doesn't show up on PowerPoint slides or in clean diagrams. You can't upload it to the cloud or hand it off in a meeting. But when it's missing, everything falls apart. It's the quiet, deep, hard-earned know-how that lives in people's hands, ears, eyes, and instincts. It doesn't have a fancy name because the people who carry it don't talk about it—they just use it. And when they leave, that knowledge often disappears with them.

Michael Polanyi, a Hungarian-British thinker, once said, "We know more than we can tell." That quote has stuck around, especially with people trying to understand what's called tacit knowledge—the stuff we understand deep down but have a hard time explaining. Think about riding a bike. You could talk all day about balance, gravity, friction, and momentum, but none of that helps someone stay upright the first time. You only really learn by doing—by tipping over, trying again, and slowly figuring it out. Same goes for working a lathe or troubleshooting a welding machine. You don't read your way into mastery—you practice your way into it.

Factories are full of this kind of unspoken knowledge, humming along in the background like a well-oiled engine. Take tool-and-die makers, for example. Their job on paper looks precise and technical: making tools and molds to exact specs. But in reality, it's part science, part art. Seasoned die makers can hear a machine's slight rattle before it becomes a real problem. They can tell if the steel isn't quite right—not because of a reading on a screen, but by the sound it makes when the cutter bites in. Ask them how they know, and they'll probably just shrug: "You just do." Their hands remember what the specs can't say.

Or look at a welder working with aluminum. It's not that aluminum is especially mysterious, but the job is full of tiny variables—air moisture, heat levels, torch angle, filler material. A good weld doesn't just look right. It sounds right. It smells right. It moves in a certain way as the metal melts and flows. One welder said, "You can hear it when it's right. You know before you even see it." That kind of awareness takes years.

Even on assembly lines—often thought of as boring or repetitive—it's not just button-pushing. Sure, some jobs are repetitive. But the line only works because the people on it are alert and paying attention. Workers pick up on little signs: a piece that doesn't snap into place quite right, a motor that sounds just a little off, a coworker's expression that says something's not right. These signals aren't written down anywhere. No one sends out a memo when the rhythm changes. But if you've been on the line long enough, you feel it.

This kind of knowledge doesn't just live in individuals—it's shared. It's passed back and forth in small gestures, quick nods, shared habits. Cognitive scientists have a term for this: "distributed cognition." Basically, it means people working together know more as a group than any one person could explain alone. In a healthy factory, work flows because people can read each other, anticipate each other's moves, and quietly fix problems before they grow. Machines help, but people make the system sing—especially when they trust each other and know how everything fits together.

Consider a mid-sized auto parts supplier in Michigan. At its height, the plant ran three shifts and produced parts for the Big Three automakers. One day, management rolled out a new software system to streamline scheduling. It looked great on paper—more efficient, more optimized. But almost instantly, production slowed. The software didn't understand the small, human fixes people made each day: adjusting timing to work around a slow machine, or giving extra time to a colleague who needed it. It didn't see how the line really worked, because the "real" process wasn't written down anywhere—it lived in people's habits and relationships. The new system failed, not because it was flawed, but because it couldn't see the glue holding everything together.

That gap—between what can be measured and what actually matters—is one of the big reasons American manufacturing has struggled. In boardrooms, knowledge often means degrees, certifications, and compliance scores. Things you can chart on a graph. But on the floor, knowledge is more like rhythm and feel. It's built through trial and error, passed along in casual chats, small fixes, and hands-on help. It's flexible, it's embodied—and it's fragile.

When a factory closes or moves overseas, we usually count the damage in job losses: 500 gone here, 2,000 there. But the deeper cost is harder to measure. What's really lost is a whole network of quiet know-how, built up over decades. It's not just that workers knew how to do their tasks. It's that they knew how everything connected. They knew which supplier never cut corners, which part always gave trouble, how to bend a rule without breaking it. That knowledge isn't in the employee handbook.

One former plant manager in Ohio put it simply: "We had a guy who could tell if a press was misaligned just by the sound of the first punch. He didn't need to measure anything. If you replaced him with ten engineers and a vibration sensor, you still wouldn't get the same output."

That may sound sentimental, but it's not. It's a real issue. Modern systems often overlook this kind of knowledge because it doesn't fit neatly into spreadsheets. When factories are treated as nothing more than costs to cut or operations to outsource, that deeper layer of expertise is invisible. It doesn't show up in earnings reports—but its absence shows up in delays, defects, and people getting stuck without anyone to ask.

Even top-notch retraining programs run into this wall. You can teach someone to operate a machine and quiz them on safety procedures. But you can't fast-track the years it takes to develop real skill. You can't fake gut instinct. Without mentors—people who've seen it all—it's hard for new workers to learn more than just the basics. They might know how, but they don't know why.

That's part of why bringing manufacturing back is so tough. You can reopen a plant, clean the machines, get things running again. But the people who once made it work—the ones who knew the little tricks and fixes—many of them are gone. They've retired, moved on, or left the field entirely. And with them went the invisible foundation of the whole operation—the stuff no one thought to write down because no one thought it would vanish.

We like to believe that knowledge can be stored on a server or packed into a PowerPoint. But real production knowledge is more like cooking than coding. You can hand someone a recipe, but that won't make them a chef. They need to know how the sauce should smell just before it burns, how to fix a dish when the parsley runs out, how the dough should feel when it's just right. Manufacturing isn't any different. It's in the feel, the flow, the small moves that come with time and trust.

Tacit knowledge takes years to build, but it can vanish in a day. It's deeply personal, but it thrives in groups. It's not flashy, and you can't automate it. But when it's there, everything runs smoother. When it's gone, things break in ways no one can quite explain.

So what did we really know? It wasn't just in manuals or flowcharts. It lived in people—their habits, their shortcuts, their quiet signals. It was in worn hands and shared looks, in the stories told over lunch and the silent teamwork on a noisy line. It was in the trust that made everything click. And we didn't count it. We didn't think we needed to.

Until it was gone.

When the Knowledge Vanished

In any system that starts to fall apart, there's a moment when something feels off. Not in a way that triggers alarms or shows up on a dashboard. It's quieter than that. A part doesn't quite line up like it used to. The weld looks just a little wrong. A shift supervisor pauses mid-step, frowns, can't quite say why. But the feeling is there. Something is slipping.

And then, sooner or later, things start to break.

It's not that someone made a massive mistake. There's no single failure to point at. What disappears isn't the data, or even the equipment—it's the know-how. The instincts. The stuff people carry in their heads, built from years of doing the work, side by side. And most of the time, that knowledge isn't lost because someone quit. It's pushed out.

Take a foundry in Indiana. This place had been making tough, precise metal parts for nearly a hundred years—parts that ended up in tractors, trucks, and factory machines. It was old-school work. Hot, loud, and demanding. The people who ran the floor knew their stuff inside and out. One glance, one whiff, and they could tell if something wasn't right. If the iron was too cool. If the mold mix was off. One guy could tell just by the color of the smoke whether the pour was clean.

Then a private equity firm bought the place.

They showed up with suits and spreadsheets, talking about "efficiency" and "lean operations." Within six months, three senior supervisors were shown the door, offered early retirement packages. In came new hires—smart, energetic, and cheaper. But they didn't know the job like the old hands did.

At first, the problems were small. A few more defective parts. A longer rework line. Then customers started complaining. Scrap rates went up. Everyone scrambled to figure out what was going wrong. But the processes looked the same. The machines were still humming. On paper, nothing had changed.

But something important had vanished. The old supervisors had a sense for the work that didn't come from manuals—it came from being there. Watching, listening, tweaking. Feeling when something was just a little off.

A former technician put it like this: "You'd walk into the melt room and just feel it in your gut. Something sounded different. The furnace had a tone. The new guys? They didn't even hear it."

Eventually, management brought in consultants. They installed sensors, updated software, tightened procedures. But nothing quite worked. Because what they'd lost wasn't a step in the process—it was the ability to see ahead, to notice early signs, to fix problems before they became disasters. They'd replaced wisdom with workflow charts. And the gap showed.

A similar story unfolded at a chemical plant in Louisiana. The plant made specialty polymers used in high-stakes products— medical devices, aircraft insulation. The process was sensitive, finicky, and required careful adjustments. Three operators had run the core equipment for over 30 years. They didn't just follow instructions—they nudged the process along, tuning it like a musician with a favorite instrument.

None of them had engineering degrees. But their understanding of the plant was deep and second nature. "They could feel what the reactor needed," one engineer said. "They just knew."

Then they retired.

There was no plan in place to replace them. Management had tried to document what they did, but the notes barely scratched the surface. New operators came in, trained by the book. But slowly, the plant started to falter. Quality drifted. Yields slipped. Then came the big hit—a batch worth $400,000 had to be scrapped after a temperature misstep.

Again, it wasn't because the new workers were careless or dumb. They just didn't have the map. No one had shown them how to listen to the hum of the reactor, or smell the difference when something wasn't right. And honestly, how could they? That kind of learning doesn't fit in a binder.

This is the hidden cost when financial firms treat factories like puzzle pieces to be rearranged. They see land, tools, product lines, wages. But they don't see the knowledge tucked into the people who keep it all working. That kind of value doesn't show up on a spreadsheet.

One executive said it best: "They knew how many forklifts we had, but not who knew how to fix them when the brake lines froze."

Here's the irony: in trying to squeeze out more profit, these companies often make their operations more fragile. They cut training. Slash apprenticeships. Outsource everything they can. And in doing so, they strip away the very thing that makes a place strong—the knowledge passed from person to person, over years of doing the job.

It's not just about age, either. Across the U.S., skilled tradespeople are aging out fast. Welders, machinists, toolmakers—they're retiring, and there's no one in line behind them. The government's been warning about this for years. But most mid-sized manufacturers haven't done much about it. Succession plans are rare. Training programs are too thin. And now, we're watching a slow-motion slide into lost skills.

It's not that young workers aren't interested. The path just isn't there. A lot of plants no longer have veterans who can guide rookies. Old-school apprenticeship programs have been gutted. And when training does happen, it's often rushed. "We used to train a press brake operator for two years," said a veteran in Ohio. "Now they get a weekend crash course and a checklist."

Some companies try to fill the gap with tech. Digital twins. Smart sensors. Augmented reality headsets. These tools can be useful. But they're not a cure-all. They can tell you something's wrong—but not why the last guy tapped the part twice before mounting it, or why he only trusted a certain gauge when the air was damp. They can't teach the habits that keep things running smoothly. They can't give you judgment.

There's also a mindset shift. These days, people want everything optimized, measured, and justified. A young manager might ask, "Why do we do it this way?" And if the answer is just "because it works," that's not good enough. Sometimes that's a fair question. Other times, it's missing the point. Not every habit is superstition. Some are hard-won lessons, passed down in calloused hands.

When that chain breaks, what's left behind can't handle stress. One foreman told a story about a pump that kept overheating. The manual said grease it every 40 hours. That's what the new crew did. But it still failed. Eventually, someone remembered the old guy used to grease it every 35 hours—"because that's when it squealed." There was no sensor for that. Just someone paying attention.

All of this points to a tough truth: you can't outsource memory. When a company moves production to another country, they ship the machines and the blueprints. But not the know-how. And without that, even perfect instructions fall short. Overseas plants might follow every step and still end up with warped parts—because they don't know the quirks, the workarounds, the little fixes born of experience.

One executive who tried to bring production back home said, "We thought we could just plug in the old molds and get going. But the people who knew how to use them were gone. We had to relearn everything. It took years."

That's the real constraint—not money, not even labor in the broad sense. It's the deep, sticky kind of knowledge that only comes from time. The stuff that gets passed along in quick chats, coffee breaks, or quiet nods at the line. The things you only know after doing the work a thousand times, failing a few, and figuring it out.

When you lay those people off, or force them out early, you're not just trimming fat. You're draining away the muscle. And once that kind of knowledge is gone, you can't just hire it back. It takes time. Sometimes, it takes a generation.

These days, everyone's talking about resilience. But real resilience isn't about bouncing back fast. It's about having depth. Having people who know the work. People who've seen things go sideways and know how to steady the ship.

The scariest kind of failure isn't loud. It doesn't make headlines. It's slow. Quiet. Easy to miss. The machines still run. The shipments still go out. But the ability to make sense of problems, to see them coming, to adjust on the fly—that starts to slip away.

And when the next big shake-up hits—a supplier fails, a key person quits, a storm knocks things offline—there's no one left who remembers how to adapt. No one left who knows how to bend instead of break.

Toward Industrial Wisdom: Strategies to Reclaim Tacit Knowledge

If tacit knowledge is the soul of a factory, then how do you bring it back to life?

There's no easy answer. No shiny app or training program that can snap decades of experience back into place. But there are ways to start rebuilding. One step at a time. One person at a time. And it doesn't start with a memo from corporate—it starts with real people who care about this knowledge, deciding it's worth saving.

One idea, surprisingly simple but powerful, is this: connect the veterans with the rookies. Call it a mentorship circle, a knowledge guild, or just "the crew." The name doesn't matter as much as getting people in the same room, sharing what they know.

Picture this: a retired machinist who spent forty years fine-tuning lathes. He's not looking for a full-time gig, but he's happy to stop by the shop a couple times a month. He walks the floor with younger workers, showing them how to "feel" when something's off in a machine. How to hear the change in pitch when a tool bit starts to wear. You can't learn this stuff from a manual or a video—it has to be experienced. Taught. Handed down.

In Western Pennsylvania, one pilot program gave this idea a real-world test. A shuttered steel plant was turned into a training center. They invited back a dozen retired mill workers, many of whom hadn't stepped into a foundry in years. These were people who knew blast furnaces like others know their backyard gardens. They didn't teach in classrooms—they worked side by side with students from local community colleges. One of those students said, "I learned more in two weeks with Lou than in two semesters of classes."

Lou, by the way, had a hearing aid in one ear and was missing a finger from a mishap back in 1981. But his knowledge? It was gold. He taught the apprentices to trust their senses. To recognize the smell of overheating slag. To test a weld with the side of a hammer, listening for the difference between a dull thud and a crisp ring. This isn't some romantic throwback. It's real-world know-how. And without a plan to pass it down, it disappears.

To make this kind of transfer stick, we need more than a few mentorship sessions. We need a backbone—a structure. Think of regional knowledge hubs. Locally run centers that serve as both skills banks and mentorship networks. Not just trade schools or job fairs, but working spaces with real tools, run by people who've done the work. Like industrial libraries, only the books can talk—and they talk shop.

Mentorship is just one piece. The next is reviving the apprenticeship pipeline—and making it real. Not a short-term internship with a checklist, but a full, multi-year experience that teaches the trade from the inside out. If states are giving companies tax breaks to bring manufacturing back home, tie those incentives to solid apprenticeship programs. No program, no credit. Simple as that.

These apprenticeships should be immersive. Not just shadowing someone for a few days. We're talking about real rotations, learning each step of the process, and building lasting connections with mentors. Germany has done this for decades, and they haven't faced the same kind of knowledge loss. We don't need to invent a new system—we just need to actually use one that works.

Then there's the knowledge that doesn't live in manuals at all—the odd fixes, the custom tweaks, the tricks that make old machines hum. If we wait too long, these things will vanish with the people who know them. That's why recording this knowledge needs to be a priority, not an afterthought. Think of "reverse engineering" as a cultural mission, not just a technical task.

One small aerospace company in Wichita came up with a clever way to do this. They started a "memory vault" project. A few semi-retired engineers walked the floor, writing down everything they remembered about older production lines. Why a certain jig needed an odd angle. What to do when a fixture started wearing out. Why one step in assembly happened out of order. It wasn't just data—it was wisdom. That memory vault became an essential tool for training and problem-solving when newer systems didn't cut it.

Sure, documenting all this takes time and money. But it's way cheaper than losing a multimillion-dollar contract because no one remembers that the anodizing bath acts up on rainy days.

Another big opportunity? Employee ownership. When workers have a real stake in the business, they tend to think about the future differently. Knowledge sharing becomes more than a chore—it becomes survival. Continuity isn't just nice to have; it's vital.

Look at a worker-owned metal shop in Oregon. Over the last decade, they've made it through supplier disruptions, a recession, and a pandemic. Their secret weapon wasn't size or price—it was adaptability. They had people who knew their machines, their materials, and their market. And they shared that knowledge, because their success was shared too. As one foreman put it, "If I don't teach someone what I know, then when I'm gone, we all lose."

That's what aligned incentives look like. When knowledge is seen as an asset—not an overhead expense—it gets passed down. Employee ownership, whether through cooperatives or ESOPs, can help lock in that mindset. It's not a magic fix, but it creates the right environment for wisdom to grow.

We also need places where learning can happen safely and deeply. Not every company can train newbies on live production lines. There's too much at stake. That's where partnerships between industry, schools, and government come in.

Imagine training centers that feel like real factories—but aren't under pressure to crank out product. Places where students and apprentices can run machines, use real materials, and solve real problems—without the high risks. These "learning factories" already exist in countries like Sweden and South Korea. Some U.S. technical colleges are moving this way, but the investment is still tiny. Right now, we spend more on marketing degrees than we do on all U.S. manufacturing apprenticeships combined. That's not about money—it's about priorities.

These hubs could also blend old wisdom with new tech. Teach machinists how to run CNC machines—and also how to listen for the sounds that signal something's off. Let electricians practice on digital boards—while hearing from seasoned pros about the weird stuff that happens during summer storms. It's not just about tools—it's about judgment.

Reclaiming industrial wisdom isn't some misty-eyed nostalgia trip. It's about staying competitive. About making things that last. And that doesn't come from software alone—it comes from people who know what they're doing.

Factories are just buildings. Machines are just metal. Software is just code. What really matters is how they're used. And that depends on skill, experience, and human judgment.

The road back won't be easy. It won't be quick. But it's doable. We still have time to rebuild the learning chains that once made American manufacturing strong. We just have to treat knowledge like it matters. And treat the people who carry it with respect.

Because wisdom isn't downloaded. It's shared. It's practiced. It's passed down.

That's how you build something that lasts.

Jeff Leimbach

Chapter 7: The Reshoring Illusion

When a politician stands in front of a factory floor—sleeves rolled up, hardhat in hand—talking about bringing jobs back to America, it's a scene that feels familiar. The American flag waves in the background, machines gleam under the lights, and the speech practically writes itself: "We're rebuilding American manufacturing." It's powerful, it stirs emotions, and it looks great on camera. But often, that image is more polished story than solid reality.

"Made in America" has a strong pull. It taps into feelings of national pride, economic worry, and longing for a time when a factory job meant steady pay, a house with a yard, and a shot at the American Dream. Politicians know this. Across party lines, these promises get cheers. Whether it's a campaign rally or the State of the Union, talking about rebuilding industry is always a safe bet. But the truth behind the applause is usually more complicated.

The idea of reshoring—bringing manufacturing back to the U.S. after years of offshoring—started picking up steam in the early 2010s. As China grew into a global manufacturing powerhouse and more

American factories closed down, the push to "bring jobs home" started to sound more urgent. The political slogans were easy to write. But behind the feel-good announcements and patriotic slogans is a messier picture.

Part of the problem is defining what counts as reshoring. Does it mean a company moves its factory from Vietnam to Texas? Or that a Taiwanese chipmaker builds a new plant in Arizona? Or maybe it's a U.S. company that buys parts from China, puts everything together in Ohio, and slaps "Made in USA" on the box. Depending on who you ask, any of these might qualify. That gray area makes it easy to pad the numbers and call things wins that may not be.

Take the CHIPS and Science Act, passed in 2022. It put over $50 billion toward boosting domestic semiconductor production. Sounds like a big reshoring win. But if you look closer, many of the new facilities aren't American companies returning home—they're foreign companies, like TSMC, setting up shop in the U.S. That's not necessarily bad, but it doesn't quite match the rosy narrative of American firms coming back.

Even when American companies do shift manufacturing back to the U.S., things aren't always what they seem. The new plants are often highly automated, meaning they create far fewer jobs than in the past. Some only open thanks to big tax breaks or special regulations—and close as soon as those perks run out. In other cases, the factories never even get built. There's a groundbreaking event, complete with shovels and speeches, but the project quietly disappears when no one's paying attention.

One high-profile case involved a well-known electronics company that promised a new plant in Wisconsin to make flat-panel displays. The project was supposed to create 13,000 jobs and be a symbol of American manufacturing's comeback. But after years of delays and changes, it delivered only a small fraction of the promised jobs—and not a single display was ever made. What started as a headline-grabbing success turned into a costly disappointment.

These stories follow a pattern. Step one: announce a huge new factory and get maximum media coverage. Step two: tie the project to national security or economic independence. Step three: use tax breaks and grants to get it off the ground. Step four: slowly scale it back once the spotlight fades. Politically, the gains come early. Any actual manufacturing benefits tend to be smaller—and shorter-lived.

So why does this keep happening? Because the appearance of a manufacturing comeback is often more valuable politically than the hard, slow work of making it real. Building factories is just one piece of the puzzle. You also need skilled workers, reliable suppliers, updated infrastructure, and policies that support long-term investment. Those things take time, coordination, and patience. But they don't make for flashy speeches.

And despite how it's often presented, reshoring isn't as simple as just moving a factory back home. Supply chains are deeply connected and complicated. If you build a plant in Michigan but your parts still come from China, you haven't really reshored. In many cases, the U.S. no longer has the small suppliers and skilled trades needed to support full-scale production. That foundation took decades to lose—and rebuilding it won't happen overnight.

There's also a lack of coordination. State and local agencies often act alone, offering big incentives to attract factories without thinking about long-term outcomes or national goals. Local leaders want to announce new jobs—even if those jobs don't last. It creates a system where headlines matter more than results.

That's why, despite all the talk, real reshoring still lags behind the hype. We've built an image of revival—factories going up, jobs coming back—but too often, it's just that:

an image. A glossy version of progress that doesn't hold up under closer look.

That doesn't mean reshoring is a bad idea. Rebuilding key industries and reducing dependence on foreign supply chains makes a lot of sense. But to make it work, we need more than photo ops. We need serious investment in people, infrastructure, and long-term strategy. It's not glamorous, but it's the only way to turn the image into something solid and lasting.

If we really want to bring manufacturing back in a meaningful way, we have to stop settling for press releases and ribbon cuttings. The American economy has gone through enough empty promises. It's time we focus on doing the hard work that makes the next promise real.

When the U.S. wants to bring manufacturing back home, the strategy usually follows a familiar script. Hand out some tax breaks, toss in billions in government grants, put tariffs on rival countries, and wrap it all up with a press conference. Picture a governor shaking hands with a CEO in front of a giant drawing of a future factory. It's a well-worn playbook, used again and again—with mixed results.

Tax incentives are often the first move. States and cities race to offer the most tempting deals—everything from big property tax breaks to fast-track deductions on expensive machinery. One favorite is accelerated depreciation, which lets companies write off equipment costs faster than normal. For industries like chipmaking or electric vehicle assembly, that can cut millions—or even billions—from their tax bills.

Then there are location-based incentives. A company agrees to build in a struggling area, and in return, it gets cash grants, tax refunds, maybe even free land or hookups to power and water. These deals often grow based on how many jobs are promised—even if those jobs never show up or disappear soon after the ribbon-cutting.

Take the Foxconn project in Wisconsin. The Taiwanese electronics giant was promised nearly $4 billion in state and local support. In return, it pledged to invest $10 billion and create up to 13,000 jobs. The state paved roads, broke ground, built structures—and then the project stalled. By 2023, only a few hundred jobs had materialized, and the factory had shifted away from the flashy high-tech displays it originally promised to build. What went wrong? Foxconn blamed market shifts. The state quietly rewrote the deal. And taxpayers were left wondering how such a massive investment led to so little.

This wasn't some rare disaster—it was just an extreme example of a broader trend: big promises, big money, and few real safeguards.

The idea sounds simple: offer the right deal, and a company will come to town. But here's what often gets overlooked—do these deals really pay off long term? Are they helping create a lasting network of suppliers, skilled workers, and innovation? Or are they just buying a short stay before the company moves on to the next best offer?

Federal subsidies and grants follow the same logic, just on a bigger scale. Instead of tailoring incentives for each company, Congress sets aside big pools of money to be handed out through applications or direct awards. The money can help with building costs, training workers, buying tools, or doing research. Done well, these grants can lower the high startup costs of domestic manufacturing. Done poorly, they just funnel cash to companies with sharp lobbyists and vague plans.

The CHIPS and Science Act of 2022 is a good example. It put more than $50 billion into building up the U.S. semiconductor industry. Lawmakers called it a major investment in national security and economic strength. And the logic was clear: the pandemic exposed how fragile chip supply chains had become, with most production concentrated in Taiwan, South Korea, and China. Building more chip factories here made sense.

And the announcements came quickly. Intel said it would build a $20 billion chip plant in Ohio. TSMC, Taiwan's chip giant, committed to a huge facility in Arizona. Micron eyed New York. Groundbreaking ceremonies popped up everywhere, with politicians hailing a new age of American manufacturing.

But getting from big talk to actual production hasn't been easy. Projects faced delays, rising costs, and a shortage of skilled workers. TSMC's Arizona plant, for example, ran into trouble hiring enough qualified U.S. staff and adapting its workplace culture. Critics also pointed out that much of the money was going to global firms, some with no firm promise to keep jobs or profits in the U.S.

Even if all the factories are built, there's still a huge missing piece: the supply chain. Making semiconductors isn't just about one factory. It requires ultra-pure chemicals, specialty gases, high-precision tools, and a deep network of local suppliers. Asia spent decades building that kind of ecosystem. Starting from scratch in the U.S. will take just as long—if not longer. A shiny new plant alone won't fix that.

Broken Supply Chains

Tariffs are another favorite move, especially among politicians eager to show they're taking on China. The Trump administration launched a trade war, putting tariffs on hundreds of billions of dollars in Chinese goods to protect U.S. manufacturers. The Biden administration kept many of those tariffs in place, showing that both parties agree on the need to push back against China's manufacturing dominance.

But tariffs are a rough tool. In theory, they make foreign products more expensive, which should help U.S. alternatives compete. In practice, they often end up hurting American companies—especially smaller ones—that rely on imported parts. These businesses may not have the power to renegotiate contracts or absorb the higher costs.

Instead of boosting U.S. manufacturing, tariffs sometimes just create loopholes. Companies route shipments through other countries to dodge the taxes. Others shift just enough of their operations to reclassify a product and avoid penalties. The supply chains stay global, and not much truly changes.

Tariffs also spark retaliation. China hit back with tariffs on American farm goods, hurting U.S. agriculture. Trade wars rarely produce clear winners. They might shake up short-term economics, but they don't usually lead to lasting change in where and how products are made.

What's telling is how all these tools—tax breaks, grants, tariffs—are aimed at fast results. They're built for headlines, not for long-term strength. It's easy to see why: politicians get credit for factory announcements, not for quietly rebuilding an industrial base over decades. A new plant is a great photo op. A slow, steady plan to train workers or support small suppliers? Not so exciting.

That creates a mismatch. Companies take the incentives, build plants that mostly assemble imported parts, hire just enough workers to meet their promises, and leave once the benefits dry up. They technically meet the reshoring goals, but the deeper problems remain untouched.

Take a car plant in Kentucky, for instance. If it uses engines from Germany and chips from Taiwan, it still counts as "Made in the USA." But that label doesn't mean much when one hiccup in the global chain can bring production to a halt.

That's the core issue: handing out money isn't enough to build the kind of solid, self-sustaining manufacturing system the U.S. says it wants. You need more than a few flashy factories. You need training centers to build a skilled workforce. You need local suppliers who can respond quickly. You need labs doing new research and infrastructure that can move goods efficiently. Without all that, the factories are just shells—nice to look at, but fragile underneath.

Ownership adds another layer of complexity. Many of the companies cashing in on U.S. reshoring incentives aren't American. That's not necessarily bad—foreign investment has always played a role in the U.S. economy— but it raises real questions. If a Korean or Taiwanese firm builds here using taxpayer money, what happens if things go south? Will they stay and invest more, or pack up and go home?

The big takeaway is this: these policy tools work best when they're part of a bigger, coordinated plan. Tax breaks can help, but only if they come with clear goals and real oversight. Grants can spark new projects, but only if they support broader ecosystems. Tariffs can protect certain industries, but only if you're also rebuilding the supply chain and training the workforce.

Right now, that kind of big-picture planning is rare. More often, each tool gets used on its own—without enough follow-up or connection to the bigger picture. What we get is a patchwork: one factory here, one tax deal there, but no strong system holding it all together.

Bringing manufacturing back isn't just about convincing a few companies to open plants. It's about rethinking how production works in America. It means building a system that can weather shocks, not one that crumbles when a port overseas closes or a trade dispute heats up. It's not just about accountants and lawyers—it's about engineers, teachers, community leaders, and policymakers working together.

Until that happens, the current toolkit will keep making noise without building much of a foundation. We'll see more announcements, more golden shovels breaking ground—but without deeper support, these projects will be more symbol than solution. A lot of hope, but not yet a future.

If big tax breaks and headline-worthy tariffs aren't enough to truly bring American manufacturing back home, then what is? Honestly, it's not a mystery. Anyone who's worked on a factory floor, tried to hire a toolmaker, or looked for domestic suppliers knows what's missing. The real question isn't what needs to be done—it's whether we're ready to roll up our sleeves and do the long, often unglamorous work of rebuilding our industrial backbone.

Resilience doesn't come from speeches or slogans. It comes from solid systems. From money that stays put. From workers who keep learning, not just once but over time. From supply chains that don't stretch across half the globe. And from leaders—both in government and business—who think in decades, not just quarters. If we're serious about reshoring, we can't treat it like a PR stunt. We need to build something that lasts.

That starts with money—but not the kind that bounces in and out chasing quick profits. We need long-term investment—the kind that once built steel mills, shipyards, and aerospace factories. This is patient capital. Money that isn't looking to cash out in five years, but willing to stick around and grow something real. After World War II, banks, pension funds, and government programs poured billions into American industry, often without expecting fast payoffs. Back then, factories were seen as essential infrastructure—not just a bet.

Today, it's a different story. Private equity often guts companies and sells them for parts. Venture capital is more interested in flashy tech apps than machine shops. Even big manufacturers feel pressure to reward shareholders instead of investing in new plants or training. If reshoring is going to stick, we need to change how investment works. That could mean creating public banks focused on manufacturing, or offering federal loan guarantees for companies that commit to making things in the U.S. long-term. It might mean changing the tax code so it rewards reinvestment in factories and workers, instead of stock buybacks. However we get there, the goal has to be the same: keep the money grounded, focused on building real things.

But money isn't enough. Building strong manufacturing also takes coordination. That's where public-private partnerships come in—not the kind that make for nice press releases, but real working relationships between federal agencies, state governments, local schools, and companies. A good example is the Manufacturing USA institutes. They're not perfect, but they show what's possible. These regional hubs bring together companies, universities, and community colleges to tackle specific challenges, like robotics or advanced materials. They pool resources, fund research, train workers, and help smaller companies stay competitive. They don't just write checks—they create real support networks.

The problem? The model is still too small and scattered. We need a bigger version with real power: national goals, carried out by regional partnerships. The federal government could set priorities—like boosting U.S. capacity in high-precision machining or power electronics—and then funnel resources to places that are ready to build. These regional partnerships could lean into their strengths:

maybe Ohio specializes in machine tools, Colorado in energy tech, Minnesota in biomedical gear. No region has to do it all. The key is to specialize, work together, and grow as a team.

Of course, none of this matters without the right people. And not just bodies in the door—skilled workers who know how to keep modern factories running. This is the biggest weak spot in most reshoring efforts. We can break ground on a dozen new chip plants, but if nobody knows how to run the fabs, it's all just talk. For years, the U.S. has underinvested in its industrial workforce. Shop classes disappeared. Apprenticeships dried up. Community colleges, often our best bet for hands-on training, were left with shrinking budgets and outdated equipment.

Fixing this means building workforce pipelines that are as serious and well-designed as our military academies or universities. It means offering real choices for students who prefer working with their hands. High school programs that lead to real careers, not dead ends. Technical schools that teach modern skills like 3D printing, robotics, or digital controls. Community colleges that team up with local companies to teach exactly what's needed on the job. Programs for adults to retrain, pick up new certifications, and stack those into degrees later if they want. And yes—

strong labor unions should have a central role, not just in negotiating wages, but in mentoring and training the next generation.

Germany offers a helpful example. Their dual education system isn't perfect, but it works. There, vocational education is respected. Students can start apprenticeships while still in school, and companies help shape what gets taught. It didn't happen by accident—it's part of their culture. If we want the same success, we have to stop treating vocational paths like a second-rate option. These jobs are critical, and they deserve the same attention and investment as any four-year degree.

Even if we fix the money, the partnerships, and the workforce, there's another major gap: knowledge. Not the kind you learn in class, but the hard facts—what we still make in this country, where we make it, and what we've already lost. Right now, there's no solid national map of our industrial capabilities. Ask a policymaker where we forge titanium or make certain semiconductors, and chances are they won't know. There's no reliable inventory of our manufacturing depth.

That's a big problem. You can't rebuild what you can't see. We need a national project to map our industrial ecosystem—just like we once mapped our soil or energy resources. Where are the foundries? Who makes custom tools? What raw materials are we importing simply because there's no domestic source? Where are the weak spots in our supply chains?

If we do this right, it won't just help policymakers. It'll help companies find local suppliers. It'll help regions spot bottlenecks before they turn into disasters. It'll let government programs target the right places and needs. There are some efforts in this space—private tools like ThomasNet or the Reshoring Initiative database—but they only go so far. What we need is a public resource: free, open, accurate, and updated. A true map of American manufacturing.

And last but not least, we need demand. Supply-side fixes won't get us far if there's no one buying the products. Businesses can't run on hope—they need orders. That's where smart government purchasing—what experts call "strategic procurement"—can make a huge difference. The federal government alone buys billions of dollars' worth of stuff every year: uniforms, electronics, medical gear, vehicles, you name it. That spending could be used to anchor key industries and create steady, reliable markets.

We've done it before. During World War II, government orders sparked entire sectors—planes, radar, synthetic rubber. That wasn't luck; it was intentional. The U.S. still has tools like the Defense Production Act and the Buy American Act, but they're often used inconsistently or watered down by loopholes. What we need is a serious, focused plan to use federal purchasing power to support domestic manufacturing.

Imagine if the government promised to buy a steady amount of U.S.-made clean energy equipment, or medical supplies, or advanced chips over the next ten years. That kind of commitment would give companies confidence to invest. Small shops could scale up without worrying the market will vanish. Bigger firms could keep production here, knowing they have a dependable buyer. This isn't about buying second-rate goods out of loyalty—it's about setting smart standards, offering long-term contracts, and using public money to build national strength.

Put it all together—long-term capital, strong partnerships, better training, real data, and smart purchasing—and you get something powerful. Not just quick fixes, but real capacity. A system that can hold its own and grow stronger over time.

There's always a temptation to look for easy answers—a new law, a clever robot, a tariff tweak that magically brings factories back. But lasting resilience doesn't come from one-off moves. It comes from structure. From a web of parts that work together. A skilled workforce attracts money. That money creates steady work for suppliers. Those suppliers grow and innovate, supported by real demand. The whole system gets tougher, smarter, and more reliable.

That's the challenge ahead. Not just bringing back what we lost—but rebuilding something better, something built to last. It won't happen overnight. But with patience, purpose, and a clear plan, it can happen—and it's worth the effort. Because when our industries are strong, our country is too.

Jeff Leimbach

Chapter 8: The New Manufacturing Paradigm

Walk through a modern manufacturing trade show and it can feel like you've landed in a sci-fi movie. Robot arms whirl and pivot in perfect rhythm. 3D printers quietly build parts layer by layer, like magic pasta machines. Touchscreen booths claim to "digitally transform" your factory with just a few taps. Flip through brochures and you'll read about a so-called Fourth Industrial Revolution— "Industry 4.0"—where factories are smart, machines are connected, AI runs the show, and supply chains basically take care of themselves.

It sounds amazing. But let's not get carried away.

Yes, the technology is real—and in many cases, pretty incredible. But the way it's talked about is often over the top. The story we're being sold is that the revolution is here, and all you need to do is buy the gear, plug it in, and suddenly your shop floor is competing with the biggest names in global manufacturing. In reality, that's not how it works. You can't just drop a few robots into a garage and expect miracles.

Advanced manufacturing, no matter how smart the machines, doesn't work in isolation. It takes people—skilled ones. It takes suppliers you can count on, logistics that make sense, training programs, clear rules, long-term investment, and a whole lot more. You can't build a future-ready factory with just shiny tools and good intentions.

There's a basic truth underneath all the hype: tools are only as powerful as the people who use them and the systems that support them.

Let's rewind for a moment and look at where all this buzz is coming from. Calling this the "Fourth Industrial Revolution" sets a pretty high bar—on the same level as the steam engine, electricity, or computers. And to be fair, many of the new tools are impressive. Smart machines, cloud platforms, artificial intelligence, connected devices, and digital twins are changing how products are designed, built, and shipped.

But history gives us a reality check: just because a breakthrough exists doesn't mean it changes everything right away. Britain invented the jet engine, but it was the U.S. that figured out how to mass-produce jet aircraft. Xerox PARC built the first computer with a modern user interface, but Apple and Microsoft brought it to the world. The game-changers weren't just inventors—they were the ones who built the systems around those inventions. They had the infrastructure and know-how to make them work at scale.

And that's the part often missing from the Industry 4.0 conversation. It skips over the fact that a factory isn't just a machine shop—it's part of a bigger ecosystem. You need nearby suppliers who know their craft, training programs that teach more than theory, investors who think long-term, and even a culture that accepts a certain amount of trial and error.

Germany is a great example. Its manufacturers rely on tight-knit networks of small, specialized firms—many family-run—that have passed down knowledge for generations. A U.S. startup, on the other hand, might buy a high-end CNC machine off Alibaba and have no one nearby who knows how to run it properly.

And the cost of jumping into advanced manufacturing isn't just the price tag on the equipment. You also need to retrain workers, update systems, change how things are ordered and delivered, and rethink your entire workflow. But here's the problem: in the U.S., financial markets are often focused on quick returns. When you're judged every quarter, it's hard to make big bets that take years to pay off.

This gap between promise and reality shows up in the results. A 2021 study by the

World Economic Forum and McKinsey looked at over 1,000 digital manufacturing efforts around the world. Only 30 had actually achieved meaningful, scalable results. That's just three percent. The rest were stuck in "pilot purgatory," weighed down by messy software, talent shortages, or supplier problems.

Take the popular idea of a "smart factory." The pitch sounds great—machines packed with sensors, AI catching problems before they happen, robots adjusting to demand in real time. But in the real world, most manufacturers are trying to hook up old machines with new cloud systems, mixing outdated controllers with modern dashboards. It's like trying to sew a tuxedo out of denim scraps. Without standard systems and workers who know both the old and new tech, the gains often turn into costly problems.

And here's a deeper issue: just having great tools doesn't mean you can use them well. A machine shop can be packed with high-end equipment, but if the experienced machinists are gone, the suppliers are overseas, and the engineers aren't trained to build things that are actually manufacturable, then all that fancy tech just sits there.

Consider a mid-sized aerospace firm in Washington state. They spent big on automation—smart CNC machines, AI quality systems, and even collaborative robots. It

Broken Supply Chains

looked like the future of manufacturing. But
they hit a wall. Their local suppliers had gone
out of business years earlier, and the overseas
ones couldn't deliver consistent quality on
time. Their engineers designed parts that
looked good on paper but were hard to
produce. And their new tech staff knew how to
program machines but didn't understand the
physical quirks—like tool wear or machine
chatter—that you only learn from experience.
That kind of know-how doesn't come from
slideshows; it comes from years on the floor.

This isn't to knock the technology. It's
to remind us that advanced manufacturing isn't
something you can just plug in and go. It's a
whole system. And for years, America has
been quietly tearing down the very systems
needed to make it work.

Take digital twins, for example. These
are virtual models of real machines or factories
that help simulate and improve performance.
It's a powerful tool. But to work right, it needs
reliable data, consistent processes, and close
teamwork between designers, operators, and
technicians. In Germany, this kind of
collaboration is baked into how they work. In
the U.S., those links have often broken down.
Suppliers are kept at a distance to protect
intellectual property. Engineers rarely visit the
floor. Workers are stuck in silos. The result?
Digital twins that are missing key pieces.

155

There's also a common belief that if we just automate enough, we can bring manufacturing back to the U.S.—that once labor costs aren't a factor, reshoring will happen naturally. It's a nice idea, and in some cases, it holds water. A super-efficient factory in Indiana might match one overseas. But that only works if everything else—raw materials, skills, suppliers, infrastructure—is also on the same level. Too often, it's not.

Look at semiconductor fabrication plants, or "fabs." They are some of the most automated places on earth. Still, the U.S. now makes less than 12% of the world's chips. Why? Because fabs aren't just about machines. They need expert engineers, pure chemical suppliers, specialized tools, and stable policy support. Automation can't make up for all that—it needs it.

So where does that leave us?

We're standing at a crossroads. The tools are here, and they're powerful. But they're not magic. To make them work, we need more than just money. We need to rebuild the things that surround them: skilled workers, strong supplier networks, solid training programs, and a culture that respects craftsmanship and learning.

We also need to ask some real questions. Who are we building for? What happens when automation outruns our ability to support it? What if we're great at coding software, but no one remembers why that weird extra step in the old process mattered?

These aren't philosophical questions—they're practical ones. Because the choices we make now will decide whether this new wave of manufacturing brings lasting strength, or just another round of unmet promises dressed in high-tech packaging.

One of the most common arguments in favor of bringing manufacturing back to the U.S. goes something like this: If we just automate enough, labor costs won't matter. It sounds clean and logical. If machines can do the work—faster, cheaper, and with fewer mistakes—then why worry about where the factory is? Ohio or Shenzhen, what's the difference?

It's a tempting idea. Automation promises an easy fix for the decline of American manufacturing. Why deal with high wages, aging infrastructure, or a shrinking skilled workforce when you can just let robots do the job? In this view, automation is the great equalizer. It erases the cost advantage of low-wage countries and makes it possible to build things in America again.

But here's the problem: that's not how it really works. Not even close.

First off, the obsession with labor costs is outdated. It comes from a time when labor made up the biggest chunk of manufacturing expenses. Today, that's often not the case—especially in industries that rely heavily on machines, precision, and tech. In places like aerospace, semiconductors, or advanced tools, labor might only be 10–15% of total costs. What eats up more? Things like energy, materials, logistics, downtime, rework, and overhead. Focusing only on wages misses the bigger picture.

Then there's the assumption that automation is a simple swap: replace workers with machines and boom—problem solved. But automation isn't plug-and-play. It's complicated. You can't just buy a robot, flip a switch, and expect magic. It takes serious planning. You need skilled people to install, program, maintain, and manage these systems. Not just coders, but technicians, operators, and engineers who know how real-world production works—the messy, unpredictable kind that software can't always handle.

One Midwest manufacturer learned this the hard way. They poured money into robotic welders and smart conveyor belts, hoping to cut headcount and win back work lost to overseas competition. But within a year, things fell apart. The robots jammed. Parts showed up at the wrong time. The systems couldn't talk to each other. Worse yet, they had let go of the experienced workers who used to solve these problems. Now, no one knew how to fix anything. Production slowed to a crawl.

Ironically, the labor they tried to replace turned out to be the labor they couldn't live without.

Automation doesn't eliminate people—it changes what kind of people you need. And if those people aren't around, or if they've been driven out of the field for decades, automation won't help. It might even hurt. Because now you've got expensive machines that no one can run, and a production line that can't adapt when something goes wrong.

A lot of folks also misunderstand where automation actually adds the most value. It's not always about replacing workers. Sometimes, it's about helping people do their jobs better. Picture a machinist using software to simulate a tricky cut before touching a $500,000 CNC machine. Or a quality inspector using AI to spot tiny defects the human eye might miss. In these cases, technology supports human skill—it doesn't erase it.

That's the bigger point. Automation doesn't work best as a way to cut jobs. It works best as a way to boost capability—when it's combined with human judgment, experience, and adaptability.

Look at Japan. High wages, aging population, tight immigration—on paper, not a great place for factories. Yet Japan remains a manufacturing powerhouse. Why? Because they focus on quality and long-term strength. They use automation where it makes sense. But they also invest heavily in training and keeping skilled workers who can run, improve, and adapt these systems.

Toyota is a great example. Their factories have plenty of automation, but they still rely on human workers to monitor, adjust, and improve things. If something goes wrong, anyone on the line can pull the famous "andon cord" to stop production. That's not old-school—that's smart. It shows that human eyes and judgment still matter, even in the most high-tech environments.

Now compare that to many American factories, where the focus is often on cutting costs. Automation gets seen as a way to get by with fewer people, less training, and bare-bones staffing. It might save money short-term. But long-term, it creates brittle systems. When things break, there's no one left who knows how to fix them. The workforce gets hollowed out, and the machines are just expensive paperweights.

Then there's the cost of automation itself. It's not cheap. A single robotic setup might run $250,000 or more when you include the design, programming, installation, and training. That's a big chunk of change for small or mid-sized companies. If it doesn't pay off fast, it's hard to justify—especially when investors want quick wins, not long-term improvements. That leads to half-hearted automation projects. You end up with awkward setups that are part manual, part machine—and fully frustrating.

This isn't just a theory. A furniture company in North Carolina tried to modernize their upholstery plant with robotic cutters and automated sewing systems. The goal was to lower labor costs and compete with overseas rivals. But reality didn't cooperate. Fabric quality varied. Seams didn't line up. Customers were picky. After a year of delays and rising warranty costs, the company gave up and returned to manual sewing—now with a renewed appreciation for the skill of the craftspeople they nearly let go.

That story says a lot. Cost isn't the only thing that matters. Speed, quality, flexibility, and customer satisfaction are just as important. Chasing the cheapest possible labor can sometimes backfire, costing more in the end.

It's also worth remembering that American manufacturing didn't fall behind just because wages were high. It fell behind because we stopped investing in the things that made those wages worth it. We gutted apprenticeships, shut down trade schools, outsourced key skills like toolmaking, and treated factories like cost centers instead of strategic assets. Automation can't fix that. It can't rebuild lost skills, repair broken supplier networks, or restore the pride and discipline that used to drive continuous improvement.

The idea that labor costs are the main problem is easy to believe. It gives executives a simple number to chase. But real manufacturing doesn't live in spreadsheets. It lives on the factory floor, where people still make the difference.

There's no shortcut here. You can't automate your way out of decades of underinvestment and neglect. You have to rebuild. That means valuing experience, investing in training, supporting suppliers, and thinking long-term—not just quarter by quarter.

Otherwise, you're left with what looks like progress—a shiny, high-tech setup with impressive machines. But when you get closer, the cracks show. It's an automation mirage: a future built on shaky ground.

At the center of any effort to bring back American manufacturing lies a simple, often overlooked truth: machines don't make things—people do. You can fill a factory with cutting-edge robots and smart technology, but without people who know how to use, fix, and improve those tools, nothing gets built. Even the smartest AI needs a skilled operator, a sharp eye, and someone who knows when something's just a little off.

The term "industrial commons" might sound academic or outdated, but it actually describes something very real: the mix of skills, suppliers, schools, networks, and everyday know-how that keeps manufacturing alive. When this mix breaks apart, the whole system starts to fall apart with it. When it's healthy, it becomes the foundation for innovation and growth. And the most important piece of this puzzle? People—especially people who are connected, learning from each other, and passing on what they know.

Over the last few decades, the U.S. didn't just lose factories—it lost people who knew how to run them. It lost mentors, apprenticeships, and everyday moments of teaching and learning. The kind of learning that happens when a veteran machinist leans over and says, "Listen to that sound—that's not right," or when a technician and engineer fix a tricky issue over coffee. This isn't just nostalgia. It's the backbone of real skill, and we've slowly taken it apart in the name of efficiency.

The damage is clear: fewer young people know how to get started in manufacturing, older workers are retiring with no one to train in their place, and companies are stuck re-teaching the same lessons every time someone new joins. It doesn't show up in flashy statistics, but you see it when a machine sits idle for days because nobody remembers how to reset it.

So how do we bring this human infrastructure back? First, we have to understand that valuable knowledge isn't always written down. It lives in people—in their habits, instincts, and conversations. It's built through trial and error, teamwork, and experience. And right now, we don't have enough systems to protect and pass on that kind of knowledge.

One way to fix this is to bring back apprenticeships. They used to be a core part of industrial training in the U.S., but now they're rare and often seen as a backup for students who aren't headed to college. That's a big mistake. Countries like Germany and Switzerland treat apprenticeships as real careers. There, a machinist or toolmaker isn't settling—they're building a respected, well-paid profession.

Some American companies are starting to get the message. In Wisconsin, one small machining company realized most of their experienced workers were nearing retirement, and local job seekers didn't have the right skills. Instead of complaining, they teamed up with a nearby technical college to build a training program from scratch. New workers split their time between school and hands-on factory work, learning directly from older employees who were asked—and paid—to mentor them. The result? The company filled its open roles, and those fresh eyes brought new ideas to old problems. Everyone benefited.

This kind of two-way learning is key. In too many places, people hoard what they know. They're not encouraged to teach, or they're worried that if they share too much, they'll be replaced. But when companies value teaching and build time for mentoring into the schedule, something changes. Knowledge becomes something to grow and pass on—not hide away.

Another important step is creating more opportunities for people to share what they know across companies and industries. This kind of peer learning—through meetups, workshops, online groups, or supplier networks—doesn't happen by chance. It needs support. It needs space where real conversations can happen, not just executives talking in front of PowerPoints, but engineers comparing notes on machine settings, software bugs, or materials that actually work.

Look at what happened in upstate New York. A group of small and mid-sized manufacturers started meeting once a month to share problems and ideas. One business was struggling with adding sensors to older machines; another had already figured it out. Instead of keeping that knowledge to themselves, they shared it. That kind of openness saved time and money. They also teamed up with a university to build a mobile training lab that brought new tools and lessons right into the factory. Suddenly, it wasn't just a group of companies—it was a real network.

And none of this is flashy. You won't find viral videos about someone showing a younger coworker how to grind a custom tool bit. Nobody gives keynote speeches about a technician solving a tricky maintenance problem. But these quiet moments are what make manufacturing strong. For too long, we've treated them as extras. They're not.

Schools and colleges also play a big role here. That includes community colleges and trade schools, but also high schools, universities, and even elementary STEM programs. The problem is, much of what's taught doesn't line up with what's needed. We love to promote coding and robotics clubs—and those are great—but we often forget to teach the basics, like how to measure precisely, how different materials behave, or how to read a blueprint. Students learn how to design in CAD, but not what those designs mean in the real world. The solution? Bring industry leaders into the classroom and get their input on what should actually be taught.

In Indiana, they're already doing this. A statewide program connects high schools with local manufacturers. Students can earn college credit while using the same machines they'd find in a real factory. They don't just get diplomas—they get job offers. And because the training is built around employer needs, it stays useful. It's not just theory—it's real preparation.

But even with great training, none of this works if people don't see a future in manufacturing. The way we talk about these jobs has to change. For years, we've sent the message that "real success" means going to a four-year college and working in an office. Skilled trades have been treated as second-rate. That's wrong, and it's costing us.

We need to show that factory work today is smart, technical, and creative. Running a CNC machine or fixing a broken production line takes just as much brainpower as writing software. We should be telling the stories of toolmakers, welders, and technicians as the innovators they are—not as background players, but as the main characters in the economy.

And we need to pay them enough to stay. If your best workers leave every couple of years for small raises elsewhere, you never build long-term strength. You lose all that accumulated knowledge. You never get to the point where someone can say, "Wait—we had this problem back in 2013, and here's how we fixed it." That kind of memory is priceless, and it only exists when people stick around.

So, rebuilding these knowledge networks isn't about chasing the next big thing. It's about recognizing and protecting something we already had. Before we sent jobs overseas, before finance took over industry, there were towns where toolmakers talked to moldmakers, where engineers and workers actually worked together, and where skills were passed down day by day.

That kind of system doesn't just make things faster—it makes them stronger. When the next crisis hits—whether it's a pandemic, a tariff war, or a supply chain mess—companies with solid human infrastructure will bounce back faster. They'll adapt better. They won't rely on manuals—they'll rely on each other.

The real question is whether we're ready to rebuild that kind of foundation again. Not just in theory, but in practice—with budgets, with policies, and with a real commitment to learning and sharing. Are we ready to treat training like investment, not expense? Are we ready to stop thinking of knowledge as a product, and start seeing it as a community?

Chapter 9: Models of Resistance and Resilience

Picture this: you run a mid-sized manufacturing company in the industrial Midwest. You've survived economic slumps, upgraded your equipment, trained your workers—again and again. You've paid your taxes, supported the local Little League team, and chipped in at the food bank. You've built something real, something that matters—not just to you, but to your community.

Then one day, the phone rings. A private equity firm is calling with a tempting offer: a "liquidity event." A big payday. A way out. "You've built a great business," they tell you. "Let us help take it to the next level."

It sounds good. They talk about growth, scale, unlocking value. But more often than not, what they really mean is cutting costs, piling on debt, selling off pieces, moving production overseas—and eventually, selling the company to someone else. Your life's work becomes just another asset in a spreadsheet.

This story is so common now that it barely raises an eyebrow. For many business owners—especially those nearing retirement—it's hard to turn down the money. But some do. A small number of companies say no. Not because they're naive or don't understand how the game works—but because they value something else. Something longer-lasting.

This chapter is about them.

What happens when a company refuses to be just another line item? What does it look like to build a business for the long haul—not just the next quarter? How do you survive in a system designed to reward short-term gains and punish patience?

In earlier chapters, we looked at how financial tactics like leveraged buyouts and dividend recaps have gutted industries that once supported families, communities, and entire regions. Now, we're turning the spotlight on the exceptions—the companies that held on, adapted, and protected not just their profits, but their independence, their purpose, and the skills they've built over generations.

Saying no to the current takes guts. It means walking away from easy money in favor of something slower, harder, but more meaningful. It often requires building entirely new systems—ways of owning, financing, and governing a company that don't follow Wall Street's rules.

Take, for instance, a family-run tooling shop in Ohio that's lasted through four generations—never once selling out, even when the offers came knocking. Or a worker-owned firm in Illinois that rose from the wreckage of a failed private equity deal, determined never to be anyone's exit plan again. Or a partnership in upstate New York—local governments, universities, and small manufacturers—joining forces to rebuild a shattered supply chain for precision optics, a vital industry nearly lost to globalization.

These aren't just feel-good exceptions. They're working models. They succeed because they're built differently. And they challenge the idea that finance always has to win.

At the center of these stories is something we might call "productive ownership." It's not a flashy term, but it gets to the heart of the matter. Productive ownership is the opposite of extractive ownership. It's the belief that a company is more than a revenue stream—it's a living system made of people, knowledge, relationships, and purpose.

You'll see productive ownership in many forms. Sometimes it's a multi-generational family business that keeps reinvesting in its own future. Sometimes it's an employee-owned company where workers vote to fund training programs instead of paying out bonuses. Sometimes it's a blend of public and private partnerships—towns, nonprofits, and companies working together to fill gaps the market won't.

But what ties them all together is this: they refuse to hand the wheel to distant investors. They don't buy into the idea that the only point of a business is to maximize shareholder value. And because of that, they hang on to things that don't show up on a balance sheet—like skilled workers, trusted suppliers, deep knowledge, and local pride.

And here's the twist: the companies that resist the typical path aren't just surviving—they're often doing better. More stable, more loyal customers, better innovation, stronger through downturns. Why? Because they're not overloaded with debt. They know their people. They've seen the cycles and learned how to ride them out.

Even Bain & Company—yes, the management consultants—once quietly admitted that family-owned firms beat public companies in long-term profits. Why? Because they think in decades, not quarters. They don't slash R&D to meet an earnings target. They don't lay off a dozen experienced machinists just to shave a point off the cost line. They build slowly and stay strong.

Still, it's not easy. The whole system is tilted against long-term thinking. Tax laws reward debt over equity. Retirement funds want quick returns. Business schools teach how to plan your exit, not how to stick around. The buzzwords of the day—disrupt, scale, exit—

leave no room for businesses that just want to last.

So how do these stubborn firms make it work? The answers vary. Some stay private and spend conservatively. Some get loans from local banks that care about the community. Some band together in co-ops or trade alliances for strength in numbers. Some just grow more slowly, train more deeply, and accept that short-term profits might need to take a back seat to long-term survival.

There's also a certain honesty in these companies. Not a showy kind of morality—but a practical one. They know who they are. They see their purpose as more than just making stuff or hitting sales goals. They're here to pass on skills, support families, and keep a promise started generations ago.

One business owner put it best: "When I look at my company, I don't see a balance sheet. I see my grandfather's hands. He started this place with a drill press and a promise." That's not just sentiment—it's strategy. It gives direction. It keeps the noise out. It's what one researcher called "memory, built into the walls."

Of course, these paths come with challenges. Growing slower can mean losing bids to bigger firms. Avoiding heavy debt might limit how fast you can expand. And choosing people over profits means making painful choices when things get tight. But the tradeoff is worth it: a stronger foundation, a better reputation, and a better chance of weathering the storm when things go wrong.

And let's be clear—these businesses aren't living in the past. They're not clinging to nostalgia. Many of them are leaders in modern technology, smart logistics, and flexible production. They've just decided not to sell out their future for short-term ease.

It's easy to dismiss these companies as old-fashioned. But in a world where global supply chains can collapse overnight, where instability is the new normal, the firms that stay rooted, steady, and clear about their mission might be the ones best prepared for what's ahead.

No, they're not invincible. The system still pushes hard against them. But they've chosen a different compass. One that points not just to profit, but to purpose. And in today's economy, that may be the boldest move of all.

Next, we'll look closely at three of these companies. One turned down the buyout game completely. One rose from the rubble. One built something new through collaboration. All of them show that it's not only possible to resist the usual path—it might be the smarter choice.

Just outside a mid-sized town in Wisconsin, tucked between dairy farms and a few fading paper mills, there's a low, quiet complex of buildings you might miss if you weren't looking for it. To most people driving by, it probably looks like a warehouse or maybe a public works garage. But step inside, and you'll hear a different kind of noise—the high-pitched whir of CNC machines, the gentle clicks of laser scanners, and the soft rhythm of skilled hands doing careful, precise work. This is Midwest Toolcraft, a fourth-generation, family-owned precision tooling company. It's not flashy, but it's deeply rooted—and it's quietly rewriting what it means to build a company that lasts.

The story starts in 1949 with Walter Laski, a machinist fresh out of the war. He didn't return with grand dreams or big money, just a steady focus and a belief that American manufacturing could be competitive—and fair. He set up shop behind his house with a lathe, a milling machine, and a promise to build something solid. Over the years, his sons, grandchildren, and now his great-granddaughter have taken over. The shop never left the county. They never sold out. And they've never wavered from their original mission.

Walk into their front office and you won't find glossy magazine covers or photos of executives on Wall Street. Instead, there's a hand-painted sign that reads: "We borrow the factory from the future." It's not a marketing slogan—it's a mindset. You'll find those words in meeting rooms, training guides, even etched into the concrete floor of the breakroom. It's their way of reminding everyone that they don't really own the factory—they're just taking care of it for whoever comes next.

The Laskis treat the company the way many families treat a farm. It belongs to them for now, but their real job is to protect it, improve it, and hand it off in better shape than they found it. That way of thinking shapes every major choice they've made—from saying no to lucrative buyout offers, to doubling down during hard times, to investing in workers the way others invest in stock prices.

Over the years, plenty of buyers have come knocking. Especially during the late 1990s and early 2000s, when manufacturing jobs were getting shipped overseas and the Midwest was hollowing out, companies like Midwest Toolcraft stood out. They specialized in small, high-precision parts for aerospace and medical clients—a niche market, but one with real value. Several firms made big offers, sometimes ten or even twelve times their earnings. One pitch, which the Laskis still laugh about, came with a binder full of luxury dream items—vacation homes, fancy cars, and a yacht for Daniel Laski, who was leading the company at the time.

Daniel politely declined. "We're not in the extraction business," he said. "We're in the continuity business."

That simple idea—continuity—drives everything. While other manufacturers were turning to private equity or going public to raise fast cash, Midwest Toolcraft did the opposite. They reinvested every year. No big dividends, no inflated executive salaries. Every dollar went back into new equipment, better processes, and most importantly, their people. Growth was steady, not explosive. But they never had a bust, either.

One thing that really sets them apart is how carefully they manage their money. Instead of treating profits as quick rewards, they see them as commitments to the future. They don't call it profit until next year's production capacity is already locked in. That means long-term planning, detailed forecasting, and setting aside money specifically to train and support their team. As one plant manager put it, "We don't buy shiny new toys just to impress anyone. We invest when it makes the work better and helps our people grow."

This isn't just talk. When they brought in robotic arms to help with CNC machines, they didn't lay people off. They applied for training grants, created new mentorships, and gave every operator a chance to learn how to work with the new tech. They didn't replace workers—they helped them level up.

One of their smartest and most impactful ideas has been their apprenticeship program. In the late 2000s, the Laskis partnered with nearby high schools and a local technical college to build a co-op for students. Teens come in during their junior and senior years, work part-time on real machines, and often graduate with a diploma and a job offer. It's a slow process, but it pays off.

Take Miguel Torres, for example. He started in the co-op program at 17, unsure whether he wanted to go to college or follow in his dad's footsteps. By 25, he was leading a team of five and had developed three process improvements that cut tool change time by 40%. Now, he teaches the same program that gave him his start. "It's not just about running machines," Miguel says. "It's about sharing what you've learned so the next person can do it even better."

This focus on people really shows up during tough times. In 2008, when the economy crashed and orders dried up, Midwest Toolcraft made a bold call: no layoffs. Instead, everyone's hours were cut by 15%, from the janitor to the engineers to the executives. No one lost their job. And when the market recovered, they didn't need to rehire or retrain—they were ready to roll.

They used the same playbook during COVID-19. Orders slowed, supply chains fell apart, and everyone was on edge. But again, no one was let go. Furloughs were shared across departments, and top leaders took the biggest cuts. One exec reportedly slashed his own salary by 60% so that line workers could stay on the schedule. Because of that, when things picked back up, Midwest Toolcraft was among the first to reach 90% capacity.

A lot of companies talk about resilience as flexibility—being able to pivot fast, outsource work, cut costs. Midwest Toolcraft takes a different view. For them, real strength comes from staying steady. They've built so much trust, knowledge, and loyalty that when trouble comes, they don't just survive—they hold together.

Their supply chain reflects that same thinking. Over 85% of their materials come from inside the U.S., many from nearby towns. It's not always the cheapest option, but it's more reliable and faster to respond. While other firms were stuck waiting for overseas shipments, they were picking up steel from a plant down the road.

Of course, they're not immune to the ups and downs of global business. Prices change, customer needs evolve, and rules shift.

But they build strong relationships with suppliers, not just contracts. "We've worked with some of these partners for over 30 years," says Karen Laski, the current CEO. "That kind of trust doesn't happen by accident."

And when it comes to technology, they're far from behind. Midwest Toolcraft was one of the first in their area to use 3D printing for jigs and fixtures. Their machines can run "lights out" overnight, with automatic inspection and feedback built in. But they don't confuse having new tech with being truly modern. "A machine is only as smart as the person running it," Karen likes to remind her team.

That's the heart of it: they mix the old and the new in a way that feels natural. They use advanced software to plan production, but their shop floor still has handwritten notes and whiteboards. Managers still walk the floor every day. They run design reviews online, but they also hold in-person meetings with pizza and open conversations. They look at data, but they also check in on how people are really doing.

If that all sounds a little warm and fuzzy, take a look at the results. Their customer retention rate is over 95%. Clients stick around for an average of 12 years. They've made it through two major economic downturns without borrowing money. And they keep growing—slowly but surely—about 4% a year, by doing one thing really well: making complex, precise parts that demand skill, consistency, and trust.

But maybe the most unusual thing about Midwest Toolcraft isn't their tech or their steady growth. It's how they define success. To them, success means passing the company on in better shape than they got it. It means offering real careers, not just short-term gigs. It means that when they call an all-hands meeting, every employee shows up—not because they're scared, but because they're invested.

Some might call that old-fashioned. Out of touch. Even naive.

But then again, what do you call the companies that took big money, laid off half their workers, and disappeared five years later?

Midwest Toolcraft is still here. Still growing. Still training.

Still saying no to the yacht. And that alone makes them worth watching.

There's something deeply compelling about companies like Midwest Toolcraft. Their stories feel real. They don't sparkle with buzzwords or flashy headlines—they just quietly, steadily, do the work. They reinvest in people. They take the long view. They stay rooted. And when you first hear about them, it's easy to admire what they've built.

But then a harder question sets in: If these kinds of companies are doing so well, why aren't there more of them?

It's not that the ideas are hard to find. The principles behind resilient, community-focused manufacturers—things like long-term thinking, employee ownership, reinvestment, and skill-building—aren't secrets. They're right there, visible to anyone paying attention. So why are firms like Midwest Toolcraft the exception, not the rule?

The truth is, building and scaling resilience in a system built for speed, scale, and short-term wins is hard. Not impossible. But hard. The obstacles are real, and they're baked into the way our economy works. But that doesn't mean they're immovable.

Let's start with the big one: financial pressure. The kind that comes from markets demanding quick returns, not long-term stability. Most business owners feel it, whether they want to or not. The pull of quarterly earnings reports, the lure of big buyouts, the constant hum of "grow fast or get out." It's tough to resist.

Plenty of companies would love to follow the Laskis' example and play the long game. But many simply can't afford to. Imagine running a mid-sized manufacturing firm that needs new equipment, better training for workers, and a cushion to ride out demand swings. Then someone shows up offering a buyout that solves all those problems overnight. Saying no might be the right thing—but it's not the easy thing.

Especially if you're an owner nearing retirement, without a clear plan for what comes next. Selling out isn't always about greed. Sometimes it's just about having a way out that feels safe.

Employee ownership offers one alternative. ESOPs—Employee Stock Ownership Plans—can keep firms grounded and give workers a real stake. But they're not simple to set up. They require time, money, legal support, and long-term thinking. And in a system that prizes speed, long-term thinking often takes a backseat.

The challenges aren't just financial, though. They're built into policy. The rules that shape our economy often steer companies in the wrong direction. Our tax code favors quick wins—debt over equity, short-term gains over patient reinvestment. Government subsidies tend to go to companies that make big promises, not necessarily the ones that prove they can deliver over the long haul.

There's also a huge knowledge gap. The kind of hands-on know-how it takes to build resilient manufacturing ecosystems doesn't live in textbooks. It lives in places—factories, training centers, local networks of schools and suppliers. And it's often held by people who are retiring or by firms that are barely hanging on. Midwest Toolcraft knows how to do it—but spreading that knowledge across hundreds of regions requires coordination, cooperation, and intention.

None of this means scaling resilience is a lost cause. But it does mean it won't happen on its own. We have to build the conditions that allow it to grow.

Some of that work is already beginning.

Take policy, for instance. Lawmakers on both sides of the aisle have been exploring ways to make employee ownership more accessible. One recent bipartisan bill proposed stronger tax breaks for business owners who sell their companies to their workers instead of outside buyers. It's a small change, but it could make a big difference—giving more owners a reason to say yes to long-term stability over short-term cash.

Then there's regional investment. Programs like the "Catalyst Corridor" in the Midwest have shown what's possible when local governments, private investors, and training institutions come together. They target specific sectors, offer support for infrastructure and workforce development, and help local firms grow in sync. These programs aren't massive or flashy, but they're smart—and they help local ecosystems find their footing.

Another promising idea is the creation of industrial trusts. Think of these as regional funds that spread risk and invest in things like equipment, training, and modernizing factories. Instead of backing one company, they support a whole region's manufacturing base. That makes them more stable—and more grounded in the communities they serve.

Government procurement is another powerful but underused tool. The federal government is the world's biggest buyer of goods and services. What if it prioritized contracts for companies that show resilience—firms with domestic supply chains, employee ownership, and reinvestment records? That wouldn't be protectionism—it would be smart strategy.

Some agencies are already moving in this direction. The Department of Defense, for instance, has started mapping out weak spots in critical supply chains and steering contracts toward firms that help shore them up. It's early, and not yet widespread, but it shows the potential of using purchasing power to support more durable systems.

Of course, not everything can be fixed with policy. There's a cultural side to this too.

We still tend to glorify speed and disruption over patience and durability. Startups that go public in three years get all the attention. But what about the companies that stick around, pay fair wages, train their workers, and quietly double in size over two decades? They don't make headlines—but they're the backbone of resilient economies.

There's an old phrase—"industrial commons"—that captures this idea. It's the shared base of skills, infrastructure, and relationships that make advanced production possible in a region. And like any commons, it can be eroded if we don't take care of it.

Firms like Midwest Toolcraft don't just protect this commons—they help rebuild it. But they can't do it alone. Resilience isn't something one company can create by itself. It's something that grows when companies, governments, schools, investors, and workers pull in the same direction.

That's where real change starts. When we align incentives—through smarter tax policies, better support programs, and strategic investment—we shift the playing field. When we start celebrating the builders, not just the disruptors, we change the story we tell about success. And when we build real connections between training, industry, and capital, we give resilience the ground it needs to take root.

It's not quick work. But neither is watching strong companies disappear, towns hollow out, or supply chains crack under pressure. The bigger risk isn't that we try and fail to scale resilient models—it's that we don't even try, and let the same cycle play out again.

The truth is, resilience isn't magic. It's not luck. It's a decision.

Midwest Toolcraft didn't resist buyouts just to make a point. They had a plan. They invested in training not out of sentiment, but because they knew people, not machines, are what keep companies alive. They didn't ride out economic storms by chance. They built their company to be strong enough to bend without breaking.

Resilience means being able to keep going when others fold. It means building with care, and with the future in mind. It's what happens when values, strategy, and capital all move together.

We already know what the other road looks like—shuttered plants, brittle supply chains, forgotten towns. That road's familiar.

But there's another one. And it starts with a choice—to support the models that already work, and to make it easier for others to follow.

Because if resilience is something we can build, then fragility is something we can stop choosing.

Jeff Leimbach

Chapter 10: The Path Forward

A strong industrial base isn't some relic from a bygone era—it's the backbone of our economy, our national security, and the path to upward mobility for millions of Americans. But for more than 40 years, the United States has acted like it doesn't matter. Tax laws have favored Wall Street speculation over real-world production. Trade deals were signed without protecting our domestic industries. And regulations often helped the biggest players while making it harder for anyone else to invest in the long haul. This wasn't a natural decline. It was the result of choices—policy decisions that slowly, but surely, hollowed out America's industrial strength.

Rebuilding this foundation requires more than small tweaks. We need serious, well-coordinated policy changes that reflect how real economies actually work—not just in economic models, but in factories, workshops, and the day-to-day lives of working people. This isn't about turning back the clock or clinging to outdated ideas. It's about creating the right conditions for American industry to thrive again.

Let's start with the biggest obstacle: financialization. For decades, U.S. policy has encouraged companies to focus on stock prices instead of making things. In 1982, the SEC passed Rule 10b-18, which gave companies a green light to buy back their own stock. These buybacks were sold as a way to "return value to shareholders," but in reality, they've become a massive drain on investment. From 2009 to 2018, companies in the S&P 500 spent more than $5 trillion buying back shares—often more than their total profits— while closing factories and laying off workers.

That has to change. Congress should end the special tax treatment for buybacks, treat them like dividends for tax purposes, and give the SEC the power to limit buybacks by companies that aren't investing in their workers, R&D, or domestic production. Even better, we could impose a surtax on buybacks for companies that aren't putting a fair share of profits back into their operations here at home.

But cutting back financial games is just one piece of the puzzle. We also need to make it worthwhile for companies to invest in U.S. manufacturing again. That means a new kind of industrial policy—one that's smart, focused, and based on results. Some people hear "industrial policy" and imagine bloated bureaucracy or wasteful subsidies. But that's not what this is about. The industries that made America a global powerhouse—autos, aerospace, semiconductors, pharma—were built through strong public-private partnerships. The real question isn't whether industrial policy works. It's whether we have the will to do it right.

A good place to start is with an updated and expanded Defense Production Act (DPA)—one that's not just for emergencies, but for long-term resilience. COVID-19 showed how fragile our supply chains are. We struggled to get ventilators, PPE, and even semiconductors. A new DPA could help us build up stockpiles, guarantee demand in critical sectors, and boost surge capacity when it's needed. We're talking about industries like rare earth minerals, advanced batteries, and other key building blocks of a modern economy.

Beyond emergencies, we should offer grants and loans that help companies build real capacity at home. The CHIPS and Science Act is a good start, but we need tougher rules. No funding for companies that keep offshoring. No rewards for firms that don't train American workers. If you take public money, you should deliver results—jobs, capacity, and innovation right here in the U.S. If you don't, there should be clawback provisions to get that money back. Call it what it is: conditional capitalism. If taxpayers are footing the bill, they should get something meaningful in return.

Tax laws also need to be rewritten to support domestic industry. For years, our tax code has encouraged exactly the kind of behavior we now regret: outsourcing, underinvestment, and parking profits overseas. It's time to flip the script. Offer bigger deductions for companies that build or upgrade factories in key sectors. Shut down loopholes that let profits vanish into tax shelters. And make sure multinational firms pay at least a minimum tax on their global earnings, so they can't game the system by shifting profits on paper.

Trade policy can't be left out either. It's been treated as its own silo for too long. The U.S. shouldn't have to compete on an uneven playing field—especially when other countries are heavily subsidizing their industries or flooding our market with underpriced goods. That doesn't mean closing ourselves off to the world, but it does mean fighting back when things aren't fair. We need better tools to respond quickly to unfair trade practices—modern data systems for import monitoring, stronger enforcement of countervailing duties, and faster action when other countries break the rules.

And yes, in some cases, tariffs can play a role. Not as blunt instruments, but as smart tools to support critical sectors. In the 19th and early 20th centuries, tariffs helped build

America's industrial base. We can bring back
that logic—strategically. Focus tariffs on core
sectors like machine tools, robotics, or solar
components—not on cheap, disposable
products. It's not about nationalism—it's about
fairness and foresight.

All of these efforts need to be
coordinated. That's been a big weakness in
recent decades—too many agencies working in
isolation. One handles training. Another does
export promotion. A third manages grants.
There's no unifying strategy. That's why we
need a new Office of Industrial Strategy within
the Executive Office of the President. Think of
it like the National Security Council, but for
the economy. Give it real authority, its own
budget, and a clear mission: align everything—
across regions, sectors, and agencies—to
support national industrial goals.

Procurement policy is another lever we
don't use enough. The federal government
buys more than anyone else in the world. That
spending could shape markets and drive
innovation, just like it did during World War
II. We should use that power more
deliberately. Award contracts to companies
that build resilient supply chains, produce here
in the U.S., and treat their workers well. For
example, make domestic sourcing a
requirement for infrastructure projects, and

reward suppliers who are investing in American communities.

We also can't ignore place-based strategies. Deindustrialization hit some regions much harder than others—Midwestern towns, Southern textile areas, and Rust Belt cities lost not just jobs, but entire ways of life. A smarter policy approach would support "Industrial Renewal Zones"—places where companies co-locate with schools, suppliers, and research hubs, and in return, get enhanced support. These aren't giveaways. They're bets on long-term value. When firms cluster, they create networks that make everyone more competitive. That's what policy should encourage.

And what about the cost? The money is already there. Every year, billions are wasted on tax breaks that do nothing for domestic growth, misdirected subsidies, and defense contracts that don't build real capacity. Redirecting even a portion of that spending—paired with smart new investments—could spark a cycle of reinvestment and renewal. The real question isn't whether we can afford this. It's whether we can afford another decade of decline.

Of course, making these changes won't be easy. There will be pushback from those who benefit from the status quo—big financial firms, multinational corporations, and others who've gotten used to the current rules. But something is shifting. Across the country, people are waking up to the fact that the system hasn't worked for them. They see the empty factories, the struggling towns, and the broken promise that education alone would protect them from globalization. There's a real opening now—for thoughtful, practical industrial reform that crosses party lines.

This isn't about going backward. It's about rebuilding with purpose. Not slogans, but structure. Not handouts, but true partnerships—between industry and government, workers and investors, old skills and new technologies. The policies are within reach. The question is whether we'll choose to use them—and whether we're ready to invest in building something that actually lasts.

For years, American businesses followed a simple rule: do whatever it takes to keep shareholders happy. That meant chasing quarterly earnings, driving up stock prices, and funneling profits into buybacks and dividends. If it meant closing factories or laying off workers, so be it. It was all justified in the name of "efficiency" and "creative destruction."

But let's be honest—that's just a fancy way of saying: strip the company for parts and move on.

The real damage of this short-term thinking isn't just economic—it's structural. When companies focus only on financial returns, they start cutting away the very things that made them strong to begin with: experienced workers, trusted suppliers, physical infrastructure, and hard-earned technical knowledge. These aren't things you can rebuild overnight. Economists sometimes call this foundation the "industrial commons," and once it's gone, the entire ecosystem suffers.

So how do we change the playbook?

We can start by taking stakeholder capitalism seriously—not the kind that shows up in corporate mission statements, but a model that actually values everyone who helps a business succeed. That includes workers, suppliers, customers, and the communities around them—not just investors. This isn't wishful thinking; it's a practical way to build companies that last. You can't make smart, long-term decisions when you're constantly chasing short-term gains. And you can't stay competitive if your workforce is disposable and your future is tied to the latest stock report.

Some countries already do this. In Germany, for instance, big companies are required to include workers on their supervisory boards. This isn't charity—it's structure. It forces leadership to consider the long-term impacts of their decisions. The result? More stable jobs, deeper investment in training, and stronger support for innovation. When workers have a seat at the table, it's a lot harder to justify closing a plant just to meet quarterly targets.

We've seen a few bright spots in the U.S. too, but they're still rare. Companies like Patagonia—structured as a B-Corp—legally commit to both profits and social or environmental goals. Others, like New Belgium Brewing, are fully owned by their workers. These businesses may not get Wall Street's attention, but they're often better at keeping employees, earning customer trust, and staying resilient when times get tough. In short, they think long-term—and it shows.

And right now, the long term is exactly what we need to focus on.

To do that, we need better tools to understand what's actually making a business strong. Traditional financial metrics—like earnings per share or return on equity—only tell part of the story. They don't say anything about how well a company can handle supply chain issues, compete in a tough market, or keep skilled workers over time.

That's where resilience metrics come in. These are ways to measure a company's ability to not just survive challenges, but keep building through them. For example: How stable is your workforce? How much of your supply chain is local versus overseas? Can your company quickly adapt to big changes in demand or global politics?

Another key factor is knowledge continuity. Is the company training new workers through apprenticeships or mentorships? Or are senior employees walking out the door with decades of experience no one else is learning from? In fields like aerospace or precision manufacturing, losing that kind of know-how is like losing a book that was never copied—it's gone forever.

The good news is that these kinds of things can be tracked. But doing so requires a shift in mindset. Wall Street isn't in the habit of asking companies how much they're investing in workforce development or domestic suppliers. But those are exactly the kinds of investments that build a future. If we want companies to help strengthen the broader economy, we need to start asking—and reporting—how much they're contributing to that industrial base.

All of this leads to a bigger question: What is the purpose of capital in our economy?

In theory, capital is supposed to help build things. But too often, it acts like a scavenger—pulling money out of businesses without caring if they survive. That's why we need a new kind of discipline around how capital is used. Call it "capital patriotism"—the idea that investors should feel responsible not just to shareholders, but to the entire system that makes business possible.

Capital patriotism doesn't mean you're against making money. It means you recognize that stripping down a company for short-term profit isn't smart—it's short-sighted. When you underinvest in equipment, talent, or innovation, you're not making a company leaner—you're making it weaker.

That's where ownership matters. Companies held by long-term investors—like family owners, worker trusts, or mission-driven foundations—tend to think differently. They're less likely to cut corners and more likely to reinvest in what matters. Their goals are measured in decades, not quarters.

Take Barry-Wehmiller, a manufacturing company based in Missouri. Despite economic downturns, they've managed to grow steadily without laying people off. Why? Because their leadership believes in building a company that lasts 100 years. That belief shapes everything they do—from how they treat workers to how they plan for the future. It's not idealism—it's smart business with a long lens.

We also have room to build on this idea with new types of investment models.

Long-horizon capital funds—or "patient capital"—can offer an alternative to short-term private equity. These funds take the long view—10 to 15 years—and care more about a company's real strength than how quickly they can flip it for profit.

Now imagine a national effort to seed dozens of these patient capital funds, each focused on industries that are crucial to America's future—like semiconductors, advanced manufacturing, or high-tech textiles. The public sector could support these funds with backing or safety nets, while private investors bring in experience and oversight. The goal would be simple: invest in businesses that are building real things, and stick with them long enough to see the results.

Of course, we have to be smart about this. We've seen public-private partnerships go wrong—especially when companies take the money and move jobs overseas. So yes, guardrails would be critical. But if done right, this kind of patient investing could shift money away from quick wins and toward lasting growth.

And the truth is, a lot of this is already happening—just in small pockets. Across the U.S., small and mid-sized manufacturers are trying out these ideas. Some are forming co-ops to share resources. Others are teaming up with local colleges to train new workers. These aren't theory—they're real solutions rooted in real communities. They just need the right kind of support to grow.

At the center of all this is a simple shift: stop squeezing value out of businesses and start building it into them.

That may sound obvious, but it's a big change from how many companies have operated for the past fifty years. For too long, "value" meant cost-cutting, outsourcing, and pushing problems onto someone else. But real value doesn't come from cuts. It comes from commitment.

It's the factory that invests in new machines instead of padding dividends. The workshop that trains new machinists even when it's tough. The CEO who turns down a takeover bid because they know what will happen to the people and the plant.

These choices won't make headlines. They won't be popular with activist investors or make it into stock tickers. But they matter—because they help build an industrial base that can stand the test of time.

If we want American manufacturing to thrive again, we need more than policy changes. We need businesses that think of themselves not as quick-profit machines, but as long-term builders of skill, innovation, and community. That means rethinking how we reward success, how we structure ownership, and how we measure what matters.

The tools are here. The ideas are already in motion. What we need now is the courage—and the patience—to build something that lasts.

When people talk about bringing back American manufacturing, the conversation often starts with a kind of longing—for smokestacks, steel towns, and the hum of factory machines. But rebuilding our industrial base isn't about turning back the clock. It's about creating something new. Today's manufacturing is faster, smarter, more connected—and far more complicated—than it was a generation ago. Making it thrive again takes more than just a few smart policies or well-meaning corporate efforts. It takes a clear, nationwide plan that brings all the key players together.

Because here's the truth: no single business, government agency, or industry group can pull this off alone. The free market won't magically solve it—it never has when it comes to large-scale production. And broad, top-down mandates from Washington won't get the job done either. What we really need is a team effort. An unlikely mix of voices and interests—policymakers and entrepreneurs, labor unions and investors, military planners and teachers. If we want real industrial strength again, then our strategy has to reflect what industry actually looks like: layered, thoughtful, and rooted in real-world capacity.

And any real strategy needs a home. A central place to bring it all together. That's where the idea of a National Industrial Strategy Council comes in. The name might sound a little dry, but its job would be anything but. Picture a permanent, bipartisan group made up of leaders from business, labor, defense, finance, education, and science—people who know how things are made and how systems work. Not just another think tank. This would be a working body with real authority to guide, adjust, and steer America's industrial policy over time.

Think of it like mission control for rebuilding our industrial engine. The council wouldn't tell companies what to do or try to run the market. But it would help set national goals and make sure efforts in different areas aren't pulling in opposite directions. If the Department of Energy is funding new materials research, then the Department of Education should be helping schools train the workers who will use those materials. If private money is backing clean tech startups, then government procurement should help those companies grow. Right now, most of these links are left to chance—or worse, buried in government silos that don't talk to each other.

And we wouldn't be the first to do something like this. Countries like Germany, Japan, and South Korea already have institutions that align industry, science, and government toward shared goals. Their systems aren't perfect, but they're way ahead of the scattered, patchwork approach we've ended up with in the U.S. Here, good ideas often die between ambition and follow-through.

The council would also help make sure that our commitments last. One of the biggest dangers in this space is political flip-flopping. A program might launch with big promises, only to get scrapped or gutted when a new administration comes in. A permanent, bipartisan council—one that answers to Congress and the public, not to whichever party is in charge—could provide the kind of stability we've been missing. Building real industrial strength takes decades. It shouldn't rise or fall based on who wins the next election.

Still, even with national coordination, America's size and diversity mean that one plan won't fit everywhere. That's why we need something more local and flexible—something like Industrial Compacts.

Imagine a group of Midwestern states, each with deep roots in manufacturing, joining forces to build a new machinery hub. They could share training centers, team up on supply chains, and attract both new and established companies with coordinated policies. Or picture several southern states forming a compact focused on electric vehicles—building battery plants, upgrading auto factories, syncing up community college programs, and working together on infrastructure.

These wouldn't be just symbolic partnerships. They'd be real agreements with clear goals—whether that's semiconductors, robotics, aerospace, or green materials. Public and private partners would commit resources and be held accountable. States already create compacts for energy and the environment. Why not do it for industry?

The federal government's job would be to help make these compacts happen—not by setting all the rules, but by offering support: matching funds, technical help, and preferred access to national programs. It's a smart kind of federalism—supporting local innovation while keeping it connected to broader national needs.

These regional alliances would also help solve a major, often overlooked problem: fragmentation. Right now, cities and states are locked in a race against each other, each trying to land the same factory, lure the same engineers, win the same grant. It's a zero-sum game that leads to wasted resources and missed opportunities. Compacts change that. They turn rivalry into teamwork, and help build real momentum in the places that need it most.

But money and coordination aren't enough. If we really want to bring back manufacturing at scale, we need to change how people think about it.

For years, manufacturing has been seen as something to avoid—a dirty, dangerous, low-status job. Schools pushed kids toward college at all costs. Parents nudged their children away from trades. Popular culture told us that real success meant leaving the factory floor, not stepping onto it. That attitude didn't just hurt the workforce. It dulled the nation's curiosity, pride, and belief in the value of building things.

That mindset has to shift. We need a full-on national effort to tell a new story about what manufacturing is—and what it can be.

This wouldn't be just ads or slogans. It would be real, visible changes—in schools, on screens, in everyday life. It would highlight the people shaping tomorrow's tools and technologies: the machinist in Ohio crafting parts for aircraft, the scientist in Arizona inventing new materials for wind turbines. We'd treat skilled trades and engineering with the same respect we give to tech startups or sports stars.

Let's show middle schoolers what a modern factory really looks like: clean, high-tech, and full of smart systems. Let's bring manufacturing competitions to national TV. Let's build museums that honor industrial history while inspiring the next generation of makers. Let's teach "industrial literacy" in high schools, so students understand how things are made and why it matters.

And just as important, let's make sure people in these jobs are paid fairly and treated with dignity. Pride doesn't come from catchy phrases—it comes from knowing your work is respected, your skills are valued, and your effort means something.

The stakes are huge. In a world shaped by pandemics, global tensions, climate change, and fast-moving tech, a country that can't build things is at risk. Manufacturing isn't just about employment—it's about control, flexibility, and independence. It's about being able to act when things go wrong. It's about shaping the future instead of buying it from someone else.

Put it all together—national councils, regional compacts, cultural shifts—and it comes down to one thing: shared purpose. That's what we've been missing. We've got the tools. We've got the money. We've got the talent. What we've lacked is a clear sense of direction, and a feeling that this is something we all have a stake in.

The real question isn't whether we have what it takes. We do. The question is whether we're ready to step up and do it together.

Whether we're willing to move past old habits and realize that our future—our safety, our economy, our innovation—depends on our ability to build again.

This isn't about going back. It's about moving forward with purpose. About seeing tools, factories, and hands-on work not as outdated, but as essential. About investors asking not just "What's the return?" but "What are we creating?" About kids in Detroit, Tulsa, or Scranton seeing real opportunities to shape their futures—not with just gigs or service jobs, but by making something real.

That future is still within reach. But we have to choose it. And we have to choose it together.